The Atlanta Journal-Constitution

AGAINST ALL ODDS

The **ATLANTA BRAVES'** Improba[ble] to the 2021 World Series

SPECIAL COMMEMORATIVE EDITION

The Atlanta
Journal-Constitution

A COX ENTERPRISES COMPANY

Donna B. Hall, Publisher
Bala Sundaramoorthy, Vice President and General Manager
Kevin G. Riley, Editor
Mark A. Waligore, Managing Editor
Shawn McIntosh, Managing Editor
Leroy Chapman Jr., Managing Editor
Zachary McGhee, Senior Director, Digital Audience Experience
Chris Vivlamore, Sports Editor
Sandra Brown, Visuals Editor
Leo Willingham, Book Editor
Tim Tucker, Steve Hummer, Gabriel Burns, Mark Bradley, Michael Cunningham, Hyosub Shin, Curtis Compton,
Bob Andres, Jason Getz, Barbara Vivlamore, Mike Luckovich, contributors

This book is available in quantity at special discounts for your group or organization.
For further information, contact:

Triumph Books LLC
814 North Franklin Street
Chicago, Illinois 60610
Phone: (312) 337-0747
www.triumphbooks.com

Printed in U.S.A.
ISBN: 978-1-63727-009-7

Content packaged by Mojo Media, Inc.
Joe Funk: Editor
Jason Hinman: Creative Director

Front and back cover photos by Curtis Compton/The Atlanta Journal-Constitution

Curtis Compton/The Atlanta Journal-Constitution

CONTENTS

INTRODUCTION

By Steve Hummer

When next you're tempted to step off into the mire of pessimism and self-pity – the very quaking foundation of Atlanta fandom – remember the 2021 Braves.

Keep them in mind and in heart as the team that forever reversed one city's sad sports juju. Rather than being the usual Atlanta-centric team that built hope 10 meters high only to execute the perfect bellyflop from the summit – think 28-3 and 2nd-and-26 and Jim Freakin' Leyritz – these Braves threw the narrative into reverse. They struggled up front, and then, the more things looked grim and hopeless, the more they were determined to win. For those looking on, wariness slowly gave way to wonder.

Remember the general manager who ordered up a whole new outfield on the fly, as if IKEA made ballplayers, and assembled it right there on the field in August. Who does that? These singular Braves, that's who.

There was the sometimes-right fielder, Joc Pederson, who rocked pearls better than anyone since Jacqueline Kennedy. There was Willie Mays, who returned in the body of NLCS MVP Eddie Rosario. And Jorge Soler, the blasting cap whose first swing of the World Series launched the baseball into Houston's inviting left field porch and let the Astros know what was what. And Adam Duvall, who got his encore here once it occurred to the Braves that it was a whole lot better for him to hit home runs for them than over them.

Remember the bombs. So many bombs. The 1995 Series champion Braves, playing in a slightly strike-shortened campaign, had no one on the roster hit more than 27 home runs. The infield alone on the '21 team contained four who hit 27 or more.

Remember the power of team. Those '95 Braves included four future Hall of Famers – Chipper Jones and the pitching conglomerate of Maddux, Glavine and Smoltz Inc. And one borderline HOFer, Fred McGriff. These Braves have one, potentially (Freddie Freeman), and another if only third baseman Austin Riley has about 15 more seasons hitting .303 with 33-home runs and 107 RBI.

This was the archetype sum-of-their-parts outfit. Or as reliever Luke Jackson put it before Game 2 of the World Series: "I think people always kind of sit there like: Oh, how are the Braves here and how is this? We pull for each other. We're a team. (Some) feel like we're surprising people, but we're not. We're a good baseball team. We're here to win. And that's what we do."

If you remember no one else to embody the unbending spirit of this team, remember reliever Tyler Matzek. Three years ago he was an AirHog, which is an independent baseball league player in Texas, not that guy in the middle seat on your last flight who dominated both arm rests and half your leg room.

He had gone to the lowest level of the game, that space below root cellar, to try to rescue his career. With the 2021 Braves, indispensable was all he was, the bullpen anchor who appeared each night as regularly as the moon during the postseason. He authored the single most scintillating relief outing in Braves history.

Seventh inning, with the tying runs on for the Dodgers in the clinching NLCS game and nobody out, Matzek struck out the side, blowing away the dangerous Mookie Betts for the third out. Then for a follow-up, he came back the next inning and retired the heart of the Los Angeles order on six pitches. If he ever buys a drink for himself in Atlanta, there should be an investigation.

Remember the team whose story was partially Old Testament, filled with various plagues falling upon the head of some of their most important players. Young star

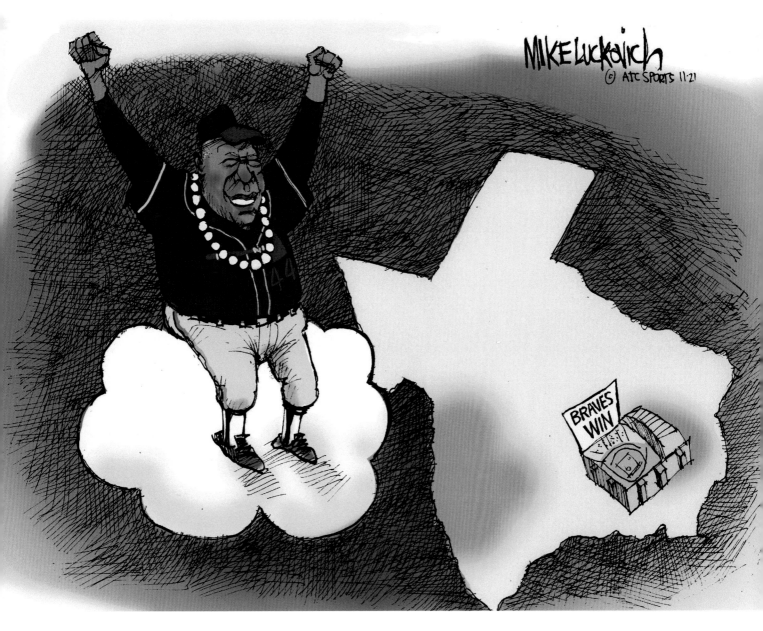

outfielder Ronald Acuna Jr., blew out a knee in pursuit of a fly ball. Young star pitcher Mike Soroka reinjured his Achilles just walking into the clubhouse. A pitcher busted his hand on a bench in a fit of blind anger. Two catchers went down the same day. Another prized outfielder was sent away while dealing with a domestic abuse accusation. Then in the World Series, a line drive found one of Charlie Morton's skinny legs rather than acres of perfectly good green grass, knocking out the Braves' No. 1 starter with a broken bone.

And then remember, the next time you catch a splinter and act like you've nicked an artery, how none of it mattered to these Braves, how they hitched up their trousers and went back to winning rather than whining. Why, just three nights after Morton's injury, five pitchers combined for a two-hit shutout of the 'Stros.

Remember the team that waited until Game No. 111 to get to the sunny side of .500, that spent four months running in place (going 52-54) before hitting some magical ignition switch and going 36-19 from there. The team that won three postseason series as an underdog. A team that resisted all the low-hanging fruit of easy excuses and delivered the best kind of championship: The one that reminded Atlanta that there are happy surprises in sports, too.

How could we ever forget? ∎

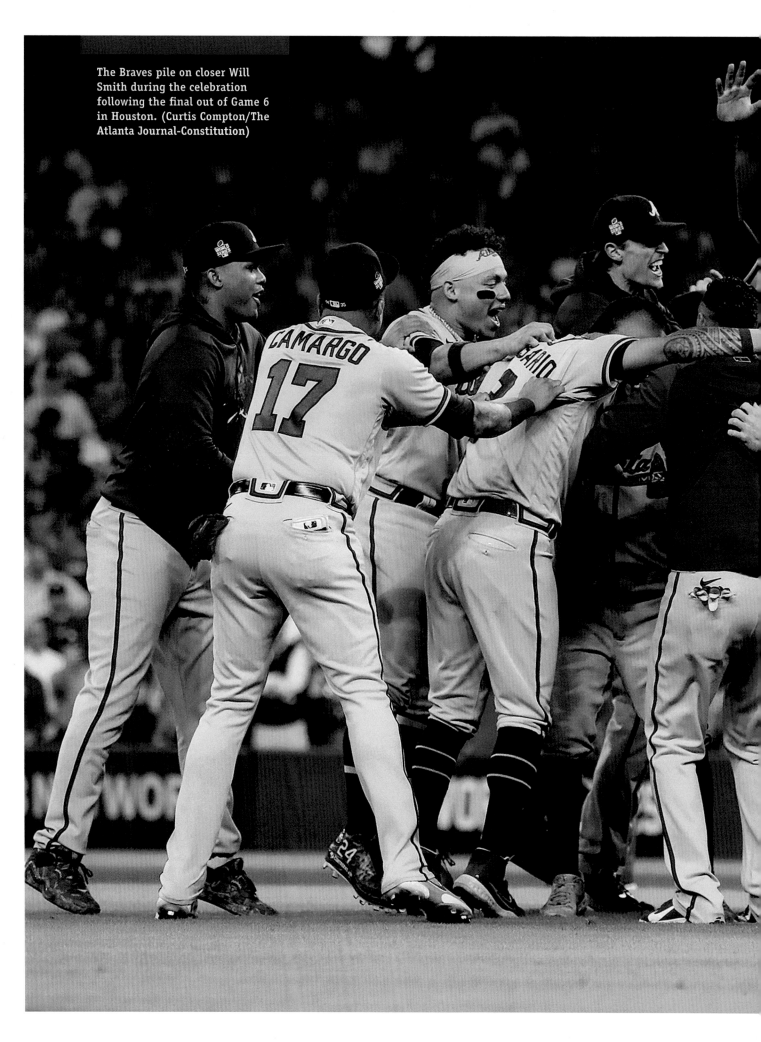

The Braves pile on closer Will Smith during the celebration following the final out of Game 6 in Houston. (Curtis Compton/The Atlanta Journal-Constitution)

World Series Game 1

October 26, 2021 • Houston, Texas

Braves 6, Astros 2

OFF WITH A BANG

Braves Open World Series with Quick Start, Ride to Comfortable Game 1 Win

By Gabriel Burns

That's one.

The Braves stunned the Astros 6-2 in Game 1 of the World Series, the franchise's first World Series victory since Oct. 21, 1996. They need three more wins to claim their first championship since 1995.

"I wondered before we got here what I'd feel like," manager Brian Snitker said. "When the game started, I felt like it was a baseball game, and you kind of get so tunnelled into what you're doing that you forget where you're at. It's just another baseball game, a really loud baseball game. Then so much happened really quick that I didn't have a chance to do anything other than that. But it was nice. I'm glad, obviously, we won the game."

The day wasn't all rosy. Starter Charlie Morton left in the third inning with a fractured right fibula sustained when he took a liner off his foot in the previous frame. Morton is out for the World Series, a brutal blow for a team that relied heavily on its veteran starter to reach this point. It's another bout of adversity for these Braves, who once again will move forward without a key contributor.

Slugger Jorge Soler, who missed part of the past series because of a positive COVID-19 test, opened the game with history. He became the first player to homer in the first plate appearance of the World Series, smacking the third pitch he saw — a sinker that didn't sink from starter Framber Valdez — into the Crawford Boxes in left field.

"I'm very happy obviously," Soler said via team interpreter Franco Garcia. "Me and my family were both very happy. I didn't know that (history) was a thing until I was told a little later on in the game. I wasn't thinking about anything like that. I was just trying to get an at-bat and just make contact."

The Braves continued showing their aggressive nature in the first frame. Second baseman Ozzie Albies reached on an infield single and stole second base (notably awarding America free tacos through Taco Bell's annual "Steal a base, steal a taco" promotion).

Third baseman Austin Riley ripped a 115.8 mph double — the hardest hit ball of his career — into left center to score Albies, giving the Braves a two-run advantage.

Soler's groundout scored the third run an inning later. Outfielder Eddie Rosario, the National League Championship Series MVP, opened the third with a single. Outfielder Adam Duvall followed with a two-run blast to the Crawford Boxes, putting the Braves up 5-0.

"We obviously swung the bats there early pretty well," Duvall said. "Doing that on the road, getting those first at-bat jitters out of the way, it's big. Obviously, this is a long series. It's going to be a dogfight."

The Astros pulled Valdez after he recorded just six outs. Of the 12 balls the Braves put into play against the lefty, six left the bat at over 100 mph. Three others had an exit velocity in the mid-90s. The Braves' punishing offense — the one that caught fire against the Dodgers' excellent pitching — tormented Valdez and chased him after 52 pitches.

Each Braves starter had a hit, the third time in their history that's happened in a World Series contest. Like a season ago, the Braves' lineup benefited from the designated hitter (which was Soler). It allowed the Braves to use Soler, Duvall, Rosario and Joc Pederson in their lineup.

Starting pitcher Charlie Morton walks off the mound with an athletic trainer during the third inning of Game 1, as manager Brian Snitker looks on. Morton was knocked out of the rest of the World Series with a fractured right fibula. (Hyosub Shin/ The Atlanta Journal-Constitution)

The quartet of July acquisitions combined for six hits, including two homers and four RBIs.

Morton, staked to an early lead, was rolling. He allowed one hit over 2⅓ innings, including escaping a bases-loaded jam in the first when his command temporarily eluded him. Morton took a 102-mph liner from Yuli Gurriel in the second inning.

He completed the inning and struck out Jose Altuve to open the third, but the 37-year-old then indicated the swelling had reached a point he couldn't continue. An X-ray revealed Morton's postseason run was over. In a testament to his toughness, he recorded his last three outs — two strikeouts — on a broken leg.

"When the inning was over, we met and talked about what's going on," catcher Travis d'Arnaud said. "He said, 'Oh, that one got me good.' He was kind of walking a little funny. I didn't think it was broken. I just thought he took a line drive off of his leg. But to go out there and strike out the next guy with a broken leg, it blows my mind.

"It's definitely a tough, tough break for us. I can't wait to see him and give him a hug."

A.J. Minter spared the Braves disaster by covering 2⅔ innings. Minter, who twice covering two innings during his NLCS appearances, allowed one run on three hits, struck out three and didn't issue a walk. The lefty prevented the Braves from burning through their bullpen early.

Over his past three outings, Minter has pitched 6⅔ innings, allowing one run on four hits. He's struck out eight without issuing a walk. Minter went from a player demoted to Triple-A Gwinnett in the summer to one mowing down the Dodgers and Astros in October.

Luke Jackson bounced back from his disappointing NLCS, recording five pivotal outs and showcasing his trademark slider in doing so (the Astros whiffed on three of seven swings against the pitch). Tyler Matzek followed Jackson, recording the next four outs. Rosario made an excellent throw fielding a ball off the wall to nab Gurriel on a would-be double that ended the eighth inning. Will Smith pitched a scoreless ninth.

"Every single person in that bullpen has a huge heart, has huge fight," d'Arnaud said. "And there's nothing more you want as a catcher is to know that everybody loves each other, and everybody picks each other up and they're not afraid of anyone." ∎

Jorge Soler made World Series history with a home run on his first swing in Game 1. (Curtis Compton/The Atlanta Journal-Constitution)

World Series Game 2
October 27, 2021 • Houston, Texas
Astros 7, Braves 2

DEATH BY A THOUSAND CUTS

Ugly Second Inning Dooms Braves in Game 2 Loss to Astros

By Gabriel Burns

There will be at least a Game 5 of the World Series. The Braves lost to the Astros 7-2 in Game 2, sending the Fall Classic to Atlanta in a 1-1 draw. It was the sloppiest game of this postseason for the Braves, who mostly were pristine in their run to the grandest stage.

Already down starter Charlie Morton because of injury, the Braves needed the best from their two remaining starters, Max Fried and Ian Anderson. They didn't get it from Fried in Game 2, although it wasn't all on him. The Astros built their lead with a four-run second inning, thanks to five singles and an error.

Kyle Tucker, Yuli Gurriel and Jose Siri each singled, snapping a 1-1 tie. The defining play followed when Martin Maldonado singled to left. Eddie Rosario scooped the ball and fired to third, but no one was covering the base. The ball rolled to the backstop, scoring another run. Fried's wild pitch moved Maldonado to third. Michael Brantley's single capped the Astros' odd outburst.

Just like that, Houston led 5-1. The inning was death by a thousand cuts: Only one of Houston's hits had an exit velocity above 100 mph (Brantley's single). Siri's infield hit left the bat at 51.5 mph. Second baseman Ozzie Albies fielded the ball and tried to get Siri at first, but he beat the throw.

"It was kind of a weird inning," manager Brian Snitker said. "It wasn't like (Fried) was getting banged around. Balls that found holes, checked swings, we threw a ball away. It was just a weird inning."

Rosario made a brilliant play in Game 1, fielding a ball off the wall and firing to second for an out. His play in

Game 2 was an appropriate summation of the disastrous inning. Rosario's error was his first of the postseason and his third in 45 games with the Braves.

Albies later committed a fielding error in the sixth, missing an opportunity for a double play by fumbling the exchange (the controversial call was upheld on review). After making one error throughout the postseason, the Braves made three in the first two games of the World Series.

"The (error by shortstop Dansby Swanson) yesterday, it was just a topspin ground ball," Snitker said. "We haven't been on this field a lot. I think that's got something to do with that. It happens. Over the course of 162 games that we just played and how good our guys are defensively, it doesn't bother me one bit."

Fried rebounded from the second inning, retiring 10 consecutive Astros before walking Yordan Alvarez to open the sixth. Carlos Correa's single ended Fried's night. The silver lining was Fried lasted five innings, preventing the Braves from dipping into their bullpen early for the second consecutive night.

In his past two starts, Fried allowed 10 earned runs on 15 hits in 9⅔ innings. He's given up 23 hits over his past three outings (15⅔ innings). He had allowed seven or more hits only once in his 15 outings after the All-Star break entering the National League Championship Series.

"I came out, and we were losing, we were down big, so I'm not happy about it," Fried said. "For me, at the end of the day, it's what I've said here: If I'm leaving the game and we're winning, I did my job. Today I didn't do that."

Astros starter Jose Urquidy, who surrendered six runs in 1⅔ innings in his last outing, held the Braves' offense

Travis d'Arnaud hits a solo home run during the second inning of Game 1. He would go on to score the Braves' only other run of the game thanks to a fifth-inning single by Freddie Freeman. (Curtis Compton/The Atlanta Journal-Constitution)

to two runs over five innings. Catcher Travis d'Arnaud hit a solo shot in the second; each of his three postseason homers with the Braves have come in Houston, dating to his two home runs against the Marlins in the neutral-site NL Division Series a year ago.

Kyle Wright was among the relievers to pitch for the Braves. Wright, a former top prospect who hasn't pitched in the majors since June, struck out the side in the eighth on 12 pitches.

"He did a tremendous job," d'Arnaud said. "He was locating. His sinker was moving a lot. His curveball was moving a lot. He did a tremendous job. When I caught him in a rehab game for me, he looked exactly the same as he did that day. It was fun working with him, and it was great seeing him have success today, especially in the World Series."

Lefty Dylan Lee also impressed despite Albies' error.

He recorded two outs, including striking out Siri with two on. Lee's and Wright's outings were notable because the Braves will need them in the coming days when they pitch consecutive bullpen games, a situation created by Morton's injury.

"It was really good tonight to get Lee in this game, to get Kyle in this game," Snitker said. "Those guys are going to have to play a big part in this."

The Braves accomplished a split in Houston. They can win the World Series with three consecutive victories at home beginning with Game 3.

"The atmosphere is awesome (at home)," Snitker said. "Braves Country is real. That's why I think it was so important to split here. You want to win two, but if you can split and get out of here and go home where we've been really good, that's a positive that we're going home on tomorrow." ∎

World Series Game 3
October 29, 2021 • Atlanta, Georgia
Braves 2, Astros 0

THE WINNING FORMULA

Ian Anderson, Braves Relievers Stifle Astros in Game 3 Win

By Gabriel Burns

Ian Anderson was pitching a no-hitter until he was removed from Game 3 of the World Series. To many, it was a maddening reflection of modern baseball thinking. To the Braves, it was the winning formula.

Anderson tossed five no-hit frames before the Braves made a pitching change with the rookie at 76 pitches. The decision worked: They defeated the Astros 2-0 on a rainy Friday night in Georgia.

The Braves took a 2-1 lead in the World Series and are two victories from their second championship in Atlanta history. They did it allowing only two hits and carrying a no-hitter into the eighth.

The Fall Classic's long-anticipated return to Atlanta was shrouded in cold, drizzling weather. It didn't spoil the experience for the 42,898 in attendance, who saw the Braves win their first home game in a World Series since they clinched their last championship – Oct. 28, 1995, at Atlanta-Fulton County Stadium.

"It was everything I thought it would be," manager Brian Snitker said. "The fans were unbelievable. I'm sure outside in The Battery everything was just crazy. It was really cool."

Anderson is the first rookie to log five no-hit innings in a World Series game since 1912. He tied the longest no-hit bid by a Braves pitcher in the World Series, equaling Tom Glavine's six no-hit innings in the aforementioned Game 6 of 1995. Only Bill James carried a deeper no-hitter, going 5⅓ innings in Game 2 of the 1914 series, according to MLB statistician Sarah Langs.

The Braves' rookie starter, who's held the opposition scoreless in five of his eight postseason outings, wasn't flawless. He issued four walks, two of which came in the first inning. He also hit a batter. But the Astros hit the ball into the outfield only five times. Anderson, who had four strikeouts, was effective despite throwing only 39 strikes against 37 balls.

Snitker pulled Anderson with the top of the Astros' lineup awaiting. Perhaps Anderson could've given the Braves another inning, but Snitker trusted his key relievers. He admitted the decision could've backfired.

"He wasn't going to pitch a nine-inning no-hitter," Snitker said. "I said, 'Ian, I'll be honest with you.' One of the things was he was throwing a lot of pitches in the top half of that lineup, getting ready to go back out when he did. I thought the fourth inning he really had to work to get through that. He had a really good fifth inning. And then I told him because he was like, 'Are you sure? Are you sure?' But I was just like, 'Ian, I'm going with my gut right here. Just my eyes, my gut.'"

Anderson understood his manager's decision, adding: "I think kind of the way the playoffs have been played and managed, you can't fault Snit for making that move. Like I said, those (relievers) post every time, so you've got to have the utmost trust in them. Ultimately, those are the guys that are going to get this thing done."

The Braves, protecting a 1-0 lead, summoned southpaw A.J. Minter, who despite a hit by pitch kept the Astros' bats quiet. An inning later, Luke Jackson retired the

Ian Anderson tossed five no-hit innings for the Braves in Game 3. (Hyosub Shin/The Atlanta Journal-Constitution)

Astros in order. Aledmys Diaz spoiled the Braves' no-hit bid by dropping a ball just in front of left fielder Eddie Rosario and behind retreating shortstop Dansby Swanson.

Statcast had the catch probability at 85 percent.

"I started charging it hard right away, and I noticed Dansby was charging hard as well, and he had his back to the ball," Rosario said via team interpreter Franco Garcia. "Obviously, we're both trying to make a play on the ball. When I knew I had a beat on it, I was trying to say, 'I got it, I got it.' I knew Dansby couldn't hear me, so at the last minute, knowing we couldn't communicate, I wanted to make sure I avoided any collision between the two of us. So I just kind of eased up on it right there."

Matzek retired the next three Astros on a strikeout and two popouts. Houston had pinch-runner Jose Siri reach third on a stolen base and error, but he was left stranded when Michael Brantley popped out to third baseman Austin Riley. Will Smith surrendered a hit, but nothing further to finish the ninth.

It was the 18th two-hit shutout in World Series history and the first since the 2012 Giants achieved such in Game 2 against the Cardinals.

"The no-hitter is cool and all, but what it comes down to is we want to win the game," Matzek said. "Snit trusted the bullpen to come in and do our job. I think Ian probably would say the same thing. I'm sure he would have loved to go out there and try for a no-hitter, but I think he'd take the win every day of the week over a no-hitter because he's not a selfish guy. He wants to win. He wants to go out there and win the World Series. And if it gives us a chance to do that, that's what he's going to do."

The Braves managed their early lead thanks to Riley, who roped an RBI double off Astros starter Luis Garcia down the left-field line in the third inning. Riley has a double in three of his past four games. Catcher Travis d'Arnaud added insurance with a solo shot off Kendall Graveman in the eighth, his second home run of the series.

It was the Braves' sixth consecutive home victory this postseason, trailing only eight straight wins across the 1995 and 1996 playoff runs for the longest such streak in franchise history. It was an emotional day from the start as the team aired a tribute to MLB icon Hank Aaron, who died in January, before the game. Aaron's family, including his wife Billye, was present. Hank Jr. threw out the first pitch.

"I got to hug Billye," Snitker said, pausing as he held back tears. "And tell her how much I missed Hank." ∎

Travis d'Arnoud points at the dugout while running the bases after his home run in the eighth inning of Game 3. (Curtis Compton/The Atlanta Journal-Constitution)

World Series Game 4
October 30, 2021 • Atlanta, Georgia
Braves 3, Astros 2

'A TOUGH 27'

Blasts by Swanson and Soler Put Braves On the Cusp of World Series Title

By Mark Bradley

The bullpen game hadn't blown up in the Braves' faces, but they were down 2-0 after five innings and, for the first time in October, looking as if they'd run out of ideas. Over the 28 innings spanning the fourth inning of Game 1 and the fifth inning of this Game 4, they'd scored five runs – two of those on Travis d'Arnaud homers. Eddie Rosario was still hitting, but that was about it.

The Astros led 2-0 midway through the sixth inning. They were 12 outs from tying the World Series and guaranteeing it wouldn't end in Truist Park. But if there's anything we've learned about the Braves under Brian Snitker, it's that they, in their manager's words, play "a tough 27," the number of outs in a regulation game.

They looked helpless, until they didn't. They scored in the sixth – Rosario doubled; Austin Riley drove him home – and in the seventh they loosed the late-inning lightning we saw in the Braves of the '90s and have come to expect from Snitker's crew. ("Never Quit With Snit" is boilerplate heading on their daily press notes, collating the number of comeback wins.)

Add this to the list. Put it at the top. With two swings, Dansby Swanson, who hadn't had a homer in the postseason, and Jorge Soler, who led off the Series with a drive that made the score 1-0 Braves three pitches in, turned Game 4 around and put this team in position to win it all in Game 5.

Cristian Javier threw two sliders to Swanson, both for strikes. Swanson fouled off the next pitch, also a slider. Javier's next delivery was a 95-mph fastball. If there's one thing we know about Swanson, it's that the man with all the hair can turn on a heater. He drove this 0-2 pitch to right field. It cleared the bricks below the Chop House. The game was tied.

"He always loves the big moments," Snitker said. "He has since he got here."

Four pitches later, it was tied no more. Javier fell behind Soler 2-1. The next pitch was a slider. "It hung a little bit," said Soler, who went down and got it, as they say. It cleared the left field fence and the upraised glove of 6-foot-5 Yordan Alvarez, barely. These Braves have wrought wonder upon wonder this golden month, but the suddenness of these homers left Truist Park patrons almost breathless.

Said Swanson: "We grinded all night, and it finally came to fruition." Yes, it had happened. Yes, the Braves had taken the lead in a game they would win 3-2. And – this above all – they could be world champions by midnight on Halloween.

The Braves had opted for an "opener," meaning a starter who isn't a starter. Snitker's choice was Dylan Lee, previously cut by the Miami Marlins. Counting these playoffs, he'd worked 4⅔ big-league innings. All have come in October. He became the first pitcher to make his first career start in the World Series. He's surely the first World Series starter to see his bullpen begin to ready itself after three pitches.

Jose Altuve grounded Lee's first pitch toward Swanson, who had to move far to snag it. Altuve beat the throw. Lee's next two pitches, to Michael Brantley, were balls. It wouldn't really get worse – Lee walked Brantley, struck out Alex Bregman and walked Yordan Alvarez – before Snitker, a man of mercy, called a halt.

"I was shocked," Lee said, speaking of being deployed

Dansby Swanson pumps his fist as he rounds the bases after hitting a game-tying solo home run in the seventh inning of Game 4. (Hyosub Shin/The Atlanta Journal-Constitution)

as a starter. "I know I'm a reliever now."

Lee left after 15 pitches – 10 balls, five strikes – and departed on the brink, it appeared, of tears. Snitker had tried to ease Lee's load by waiting until he arrived at the ballpark Saturday to inform him he'd be starting Game 4 of the 2021 World Series. In the end, his 15-pitch stint did no great harm: Altuve scored on a Carlos Correa groundout after Kyle Wright entered. That was the extent of the damage. Still, the Braves trailed in a Series that hadn't seen a lead change. (It has now.)

Wright, the former first-round draftee who won the clinching game against Miami in the 2020 Division Series, had worked two big-league games this season. He had, however, slipped onto the World Series roster. In the Game 2 loss, he struck out the side in the eighth. He was the guy the Braves had targeted for the heavy work in Game 4, and he did his job. He went 4⅔ innings, allowing only one run – an Altuve homer in the fourth. Wright – and Lee, in a way – kept the Braves in it.

"I'm so proud of Kyle," Snitker said. "He probably doesn't know what he did for us tonight."

Game 4 also was a bullpen game for the Astros, sort of. Zack Greinke is bound for the Hall of Fame. He's also a 38-year-old pitcher on whom Houston wasn't sure it could rely. But he'd worked 3,209 career innings, and he tacked on four scoreless ones this night. The Braves put men aboard, but twice they hit into double plays. The game wasn't nearly over, though it was trending in the wrong direction.

Then Swanson and Soler put it right, and the first-string bullpen – Luke Jackson in the eighth, Will Smith in the ninth – kept it there. Oh, and Rosario made another outrageous play, tracking down Altuve's drive off Jackson to end the eighth. "It's unbelievable what I was doing tonight," Rosario said afterward, laughing as he spoke. "Wow, what a catch!"

Said Soler, watching from the dugout: "We all looked at each other in amazement."

Said Rosario: "It just happened. That's it. I threw my glove at it."

Said Snitker: "I'm not even going to look at it again. That's not something we put in our instructional videos."

These Incredibles are 27 outs from being world champs, though all who know Atlanta's sports history are aware that even the surest thing is never sure. "I think they'll handle it fine," said Snitker, speaking of the weight on this team to bring this city a title.

Yes, we're forever forlorn Atlanta, but these Braves have, for a while now, seemed different. They're looser. They play hard for each other. And here they stand, having won the most dramatic game of a white-knuckle postseason.

One win to go. One lousy win. ■

Jorge Soler hits a pinch-hit home run to give the Braves a 3-2 lead in Game 4. (Curtis Compton/The Atlanta Journal-Constitution)

World Series Game 5
October 31, 2021 • Atlanta, Georgia
Astros 9, Braves 5

ALL TRICK & NO TREAT
Braves Take Early Lead but Can't Finish Off Astros in Game 5
By Gabriel Burns

The Braves looked headed for their second championship in Atlanta history with Adam Duvall's thunderous first-inning swing. But their pitching finally faltered, and the World Series is returning to Houston.

After squandering 4-0 and 5-4 leads, the Braves fell to the Astros 9-5 on Halloween at Truist Park. There was no treat for the 43,122 fans in attendance, who saw the Braves lose at home for the first time this postseason.

While they still lead the World Series 3-2, the Braves can only win the championship in Houston, the site of Games 6 and 7.

"They're not going to quit," Duvall said. "They're not going to roll over. We're playing for it all. We're playing for everything right now. We're playing for the dreams that we've had as a little kid. It's not going to be easy. This time of the year, all throughout the postseason it's not going to be easy. You've got guys that are willing to run through walls for a win. We've got an off day, travel day, and we'll turn the page and get back at them."

The night couldn't have started more promising. Duvall smacked a grand slam off Framber Valdez to put the Braves up 4-0 in the first inning. But the Braves couldn't protect the early advantage. Houston tied the game by the completion of the top of the third.

Rookie Tucker Davidson started for the Braves, whose good fortune in bullpen games finally expired. He gave up two runs in the second, cutting the Braves' lead in half, before Houston reset the game in the third. Shortstop Dansby Swanson, so steady for the Braves all season, committed his second error of the series when he botched a grounder from Jose Altuve to open the frame.

Davidson then walked Michael Brantley, leading manager Brian Snitker to make a pitching change. Carlos Correa greeted Braves reliever Jesse Chavez with an RBI double. Yuli Gurriel's groundout tied the game.

First baseman Freddie Freeman put the Braves back ahead with a homer – his first in the World Series – in the bottom of the inning. But Freeman's team didn't score again.

The Astros spoiled the Braves' night with a five-run fifth. Lefty A.J. Minter surrendered three hits and walked two (one intentional) in the inning. Correa and Gurriel singled. With two down, the Braves intentionally walked Alex Bregman to bring up Martin Maldonado.

Minter walked Maldonado on five pitches, tying the game. Marwin Gonzalez's pinch-hit single scored another run and ended Minter's night. The damage was done.

"I wouldn't even call it a bad outing," Minter said. "I felt my stuff was just as sharp tonight as it was in other outings. I felt like I was 1-2, 0-2 on every hitter. Those guys made quality swings on two strikes. I guess I could have made some better pitches with two strikes. … For me, it was just I tried to aim the ball instead of just driving it to the mitt. That's obviously the one thing I would take back."

A triumphant Adam Duvall rounds first base as first base coach Eric Young Sr. celebrates following Duvall's grand slam that gave the Braves a 4-0 lead in the first inning of Game 5. (Curtis Compton/The Atlanta Journal-Constitution)

And then a shot to score two runs, just like that.

"I'm not worried about it. I've been pitching good and feeling good. And I'm still feeling good. I'll be ready to go Game 6."

After the third inning, the Braves managed three hits. They had only one runner reach scoring position – a two-out double from third baseman Austin Riley in the fifth. The Astros, meanwhile, had an awaited offensive awakening to send the series back to Texas. Houston pounded out 12 hits, nine of which were singles. They were 1-for-23 with runners in scoring position against Braves relievers entering the night; they had four such hits Sunday. They became the fourth team to come back from a deficit of four or more runs in a World Series game.

Braves relievers Tyler Matzek, Luke Jackson and Will Smith will have two days rest before Game 6 after not pitching in Game 5. Chris Martin gave the Braves 1⅓ scoreless frames while Drew Smyly covered the final three innings, allowing two runs on five hits.

The Braves' bid at winning the World Series in front of their fans ended with a thud. It was their first home loss of the postseason (7-1). They fell one win short of tying the home postseason winning streak record set by the 1995 club.

"It would have been great (to win it at home)," Snitker said. "I'll take it anywhere. I don't care where we're at. If we win the World Series, it doesn't matter where it is. I'd have loved to have done it in front of our fans. Hopefully, we can do it the next couple of days."

The Braves have Max Fried and, if necessary, Ian Anderson ready for the next two games, but Game 5 will sting. Charlie Morton, who broke his leg in Game 1, would've started the game rather than Davidson and the parade of Braves relievers.

Fried will start for the Braves in Game 6. The Astros will bring back Luis Garcia on short rest.

"I always feel good when Max pitches," Snitker said. "He always gives you a chance to win. Our bullpen's in good shape. Max has got full rest and we should be good to go." ∎

Ozzie Albies slides safely into third base during the Braves' four-run first inning. (Hyosub Shin/The Atlanta Journal-Constitution)

World Series Game 6
November 2, 2021 • Houston, Texas
Braves 7, Astros 0

FROM MEDIOCRE TO MAJESTIC!

Braves Blank Astros, Cap Amazing World Series Run in Style

By Mark Bradley

On April 2, they had a losing record. On June 2, they had a losing record. On Aug. 2, they had a losing record.

On Nov. 2, they became world champions.

The Braves, who'd become a running joke for their inability to get it right in the postseason, completed one of the most astonishing runs the grand old game has ever seen, winning Game 6 by a landslide – final score: 7-0 – and the World Series 4-2. They did it behind Max Fried, a pitcher who was 1 year, 9 months and 10 days old when the Atlanta Braves claimed their first championship. (Another lefty won Game 6 on Oct. 28, 1995 – Tom Glavine.)

They did it with Jorge Soler, who became a Brave on July 30, staring down Luis Garcia, the Astros' starting pitcher working on short rest. Garcia struck out Soler in the first inning with a cutter. When the two faced one another again, Garcia was near the end. Soler locked on to everything. He ripped a slider foul down the third-base line. He did the same with a four-seam fastball. On the eighth pitch of the at-bat, Garcia's 42nd and last of the night, there came another cutter.

Soler sent it screaming across the sky. It carried far beyond the Crawford Boxes in left field, landing on the train track that the Astros' little choo-choo traverses. Exit velocity: 109.6 mph. Distance: 446 feet. Impact: incalculable.

"I was sitting on something offspeed," Soler said, speaking through translator Franco Garcia. "I didn't want what happened when I struck out the first time."

The Braves led 3-0. Yeah, they'd led 4-0 in Game 5 on Adam Duvall's grand slam. This was different. The Braves weren't trying to make do with an "opener." This time, the Astros had to deal with Fried, who after a dicey first inning morphed into Mad Max.

Fried was coming off two disappointing starts. This didn't begin well, either. Jose Altuve beat out a grounder to shortstop. Michael Brantley reached on Fried's error – he missed the first-base bag after gloving Freddie Freeman's toss – and stepped on the pitcher's ankle in the process. Charlie Morton had been lost to a broken leg in Game 1. Had the Braves lost Fried, too?

Fried performed some stretches. He did a few little jumps. He resumed work with two men on and nobody out. He struck out Carlos Correa on a slider, induced Yordan Alvarez to ground out and got Yuli Gurriel looking on a 95-mph fastball. As he walked toward the dugout, Fried – not a rah-rah guy – gave a shout.

The Astros managed leadoff singles in the third and fourth; they were overridden by double plays. Fried needed only 40 pitches to get through four innings. He had his lead. He wasn't giving it back. He exited after six innings, his team leading by a touchdown. He threw 74 pitches, 50 for strikes.

"You saw the real Max Fried tonight," Freeman said. "He had a chip on his shoulder after the last two outings."

Of the 10 teams that qualified for the playoffs, the

Jorge Soler holds the World Series Most Valuable Player Trophy after Game 6. Soler won the award after hitting three home runs in the series. (Curtis Compton/The Atlanta Journal-Constitution)

Braves had the 10th-best record. They crept into October because nobody else in the National League East could build a lead big enough to withstand the makeover the Braves gave themselves at the trade deadline, when general manager Alex Anthopoulos added four outfielders, each of whom made a difference.

Joc Pederson, wearer of pearls, hit the home run that won Game 3 of the Division Series. Eddie Rosario, MVP of the League Championship Series against the Dodgers, has rebranded himself as Super Rosario. Duvall had two homers and six RBIs in the World Series.

And Soler? He missed the NLCS after testing positive for COVID-19. He led off the Fall Classic with a home run. As a pinch-hitter, he won the stunning Game 4 with another. He returned to the city of NASA and launched a moonshot. He'd started the season as a Cub. He ended it as World Series MVP.

As Freeman, the franchise cornerstone, said: "We hit every pothole you could possibly hit, but the car kept running all the way to the World Series."

Game 6 got merrier as it went. Dansby Swanson hit another home run off poor Cristian Javier, who'd yielded the back-to-back blasts from Swanson and Soler that made this Series the Braves' to lose. Ozzie Albies, dropped from third in the order to seventh, reached base three times and scored twice. Freeman doubled off the wall in left-center to make it 6-0 in the fifth. Just for the heck of it, he homered in the seventh.

Anyone feeling the urge to mention 28-3 and lost leads in Houston drew no laughs. The Braves weren't losing this. These Braves were not those Falcons.

Said Swanson: "I was here in Houston when the Falcons lost the Super Bowl. No better story could be written than us winning the World Series in Houston."

Never has a team that didn't climb over .500 until Aug. 5 made the postseason, let alone won it all. En route, the Braves beat the Brewers, who won 95 games; the Dodgers, who won 106, and now the Astros, who won 95. The Braves trailed only in the Division Series. They didn't face an elimination game. They were 11-5 in the postseason, which is a winning percentage of .688, which over a 162-game season would mean 111 wins, which would be a stamp of greatness.

That's what we saw this postseason. A team that spent four months failing to break .500; a team without Ronald Acuna,

Max Fried held the Astros scoreless for six innings in Game 6, throwing just 74 pitches. (Curtis Compton/The Atlanta Journal-Constitution)

its most gifted player, and Mike Soroka, its most gifted pitcher; a team that might have been a deadline seller had its GM not been determined to wring everything possible from a season going nowhere … that modest bunch rose up and touched greatness when it mattered most, which is the reverse of recent Braves (and Atlanta) history.

Not that Anthopoulos saw this coming. Nobody saw this coming. He made his moves because the East was still winnable, and any team that reaches the playoffs has a theoretical chance to win the World Series. This team, of all teams, rendered the theoretical a reality. Of the 23 Atlanta-era Braves teams to play in the postseason, this one had the second-worst record. This team, of all teams, is a champion.

Said Freeman, who recorded the final out on Swanson's throw: "I'm numb. I'm talking to you all about how it feels, but I'm really not feeling anything yet … You probably saw me put the ball in my back pocket right then."

Said third baseman Austin Riley, speaking before Game 6: "We were searching. There's no question about that. If you asked me, I was like, 'A lot of things have to go right for (postseason success) to happen,' and it has. We've made a lot of moves to make it happen. Going through those struggles is what made us bond together as a team. We're super close. What's gotten us here is just that bond we have as a team. We believe in each other. I think that goes a long way."

Then: "You play in this game to be in the World Series, to win a World Series championship. The competitive mind-set of a baseball player is that you don't ever doubt that. You always think there's a chance. This game is crazy, and I think everyone sees a lot of crazy things can happen."

A crazy thing just happened, though it doesn't seem crazy if you've been watching. The 2021 Braves went from being nothing special to being the best team in this tournament by some distance. There was no reason for this to happen, no reason except a GM's diligence and a 66-year-old manager's steady hand and a bunch of guys who coalesced in a way that will forever defy belief. This franchise will win more titles. It will never win another this much fun. ■

Freddie Freeman celebrates after hitting a solo home run in the seventh inning of Game 6. (Curtis Compton/The Atlanta Journal-Constitution)

ROAD TO
THE TITLE

FIRST BASEMAN

5

FREDDIE FREEMAN

Chipper Jones Reminds Freddie Freeman: 'You're Still Missing One Thing'

By Gabriel Burns · March 2, 2021

Braves first baseman Freddie Freeman needs plenty of space to store his awards. He's coming off a season in which he won National League MVP, the Hank Aaron Award and other honors. It was one of the great individual seasons in Braves history.

Yet Freeman is missing one notable achievement on his resume.

Hall of Famer and Braves coach Chipper Jones provided a reminder of that, according to Freeman. Jones, one of the franchise's biggest icons, was the team's most recent MVP (1999) until Freeman last season. But Jones also was part of the Braves' most recent world championship, in 1995.

These Braves have won the NL East three consecutive seasons, but they haven't been the last team standing in October. They came closer than the organization had in two decades last postseason, but ultimately fell to the eventual champion Dodgers in Game 7 of the NL Championship Series.

The individual awards are nice, but Freeman, entering his 12th season with the Braves, is one piece of jewelry short.

"I was talking to Chipper, and he said, 'You've got every award now, but you're still missing one thing,'" Freeman said. "I said, 'Yep. I know it. And I'm coming for it.' We're getting closer and closer. We have the right team, the right personnel, the right coaching staff and the right front office. We're set up perfectly to achieve goals here. I can probably match Chipper in pretty much everything here and get that World Series ring. ... The awards don't change anything. I have one goal and that's to win the World Series."

The 2021 Braves might offer Freeman's best chance to date. They return the core of the 2020 team along with more internal growth and veteran rotation upgrades. If the Braves finally break through this postseason, Freeman undoubtedly will be at the center of it all. And his legacy would change forever because of it. ∎

First baseman Freddie Freeman has accomplished just about everything on an individual level during his illustrious MLB career, but as reminded by fellow franchise legend Chipper Jones, Freeman entered the 2021 season still seeking his first World Series title. (Curtis Compton/The Atlanta Journal-Constitution)

Freddie Freeman's impending free agency was a storyline early in the 2021 season, but the shift quickly focused to the task at hand, primarily winning the fourth championship in team history. (Curtis Compton/The Atlanta Journal-Constitution)

RELOCATED

MLB Moves All-Star Game Out of Georgia Over Voting Law

By Tim Tucker, Greg Bluestein and Stephen Deere • April 2, 2021

Major League Baseball decided April 2 that it would move the 2021 All-Star game, a high-profile event that had been scheduled for Truist Park in July, out of Georgia in response to the state's new voting law.

MLB Commissioner Rob Manfred made the decision eight days after Gov. Brian Kemp signed the sweeping elections overhaul into law amid fierce opposition from Democrats and voting rights activists.

"I have decided that the best way to demonstrate our values as a sport is by relocating this year's All-Star game," Manfred said. "Major League Baseball fundamentally supports voting rights for all Americans and opposes restrictions to the ballot box."

The push to move the game had gathered momentum after several large corporations condemned the new law and President Joe Biden said he would "strongly support" relocating the event.

Kemp, who two years ago participated in a ceremony awarding the All-Star festivities to Atlanta, blasted MLB's decision.

"Major League Baseball caved to fear, political opportunism and liberal lies," Kemp said in a statement. "Georgians — and all Americans — should fully understand what MLB's knee-jerk decision means: cancel culture and woke political activists are coming for every aspect of your life, sports included."

Atlanta Mayor Keisha Lance Bottoms predicted baseball's decision is "likely the first of many dominoes to fall, until the unnecessary barriers put in place to restrict access to the ballot box are removed."

Manfred's announcement ended several years of planning by the Braves to host the All-Star game and related activities. The Braves were "deeply disappointed" by MLB's action.

"This was neither our decision nor our recommendation, and we are saddened that fans will not be able to see this event in our city," the Braves said in a statement. "The Braves organization will continue to stress the importance of equal voting opportunities, and we had hoped our city could use this event as a platform to enhance the discussion. Our city has always been known as a uniter in divided times, and we will miss the opportunity to address issues that are important to our community.

"Unfortunately, businesses, employees and fans in Georgia are the victims of this decision."

Manfred said that his office had "thoughtful conversations" with teams, current and former players, the MLB Players Association, the Players Alliance and others about moving the game. Tony Clark, executive director of the Players Association, had said last week that the union wanted to discuss the possibility.

Cobb Chairwoman Lisa Cupid said she was disappointed to learn of MLB's decision, but she understood it.

Cupid said she appealed to Clark during a phone conversation to help keep the All-Star game in her home county because Cobb businesses were in desperate need of the dollars it would bring.

"We certainly would have been uplifted had they chose to stay here," Cupid said. "Recognizing that we are in a pandemic, this would have given us a lift out of that."

Cupid said MLB's move highlights the need for her and other Cobb officials and business leaders to send a message to state lawmakers "that we can do better as a state to showcase that we are an open and inviting county that not only values our visitors, but that we value our residents and our voters."

Democratic state Rep. Teri Anulewicz, who represents Smyrna and the Truist Park area in the Legislature, also expressed disappointment the game was moved. "At the same time, I absolutely understand the disgust and frustration with our leadership in Georgia that ultimately led to this decision," she said.

Stacey Abrams, voting rights activist and former gubernatorial candidate, said she, too, was disappointed in MLB's decision to relocate the game, but proud of its stance on voting rights. She urged events and productions to "come and speak out or stay and fight."

Kemp, in his statement, called losing the event "the

A hotly debated issue throughout Georgia and MLB, the 2021 All-Star Game was moved out of Atlanta and ultimately took place in Denver. (John Spink/The Atlanta Journal-Constitution)

direct result of repeated lies from Joe Biden and Stacey Abrams about a bill that expands access to the ballot box and ensures the integrity of our elections."

"I will not back down," Kemp said. "Georgians will not be bullied."

Said former U.S. Sen. Kelly Loeffler, who started a GOP-leaning voter mobilization group called Greater Georgia after her January defeat: "It's extremely unfortunate that MLB has fallen into the woke misinformation campaign being spread by Democrats — only to the detriment of hardworking Georgians and small businesses."

The state's new far-ranging elections law includes a new ID requirement for mail-in votes, curbs the use of ballot drop boxes and gives the Republican-controlled Legislature more power over local elections officials. It also bans volunteers from handing out food and water to voters waiting in lines and expands weekend voting in some rural counties.

Kemp and other supporters say the overhaul will increase confidence in Georgia's voting system. Democrats and voting rights advocates say the restrictions in the new law aim to suppress turnout from voters of color after November and January elections ended in GOP defeats in Georgia, once a reliably Republican state.

Left-leaning organizations have filed four lawsuits asking federal judges to declare the law an unconstitutional violation of the Voting Rights Act.

The Braves and Cobb County began pursuing an All-Star game as soon as the stadium opened in 2017 and were officially awarded the 2021 event amid great fanfare in 2019.

"We are deeply saddened and very disappointed with the decision to move the (game)," Sharon Mason, Cobb Chamber president and CEO, said. "Our county, region and state were excited and ready to host fans and experience our community with many events planned.

"This decision will have a negative impact on the frontline workers and local businesses located around Truist Park and our region that were looking forward to the economic boost from these events. It is important that we support our local businesses now more than ever."

Georgia companies and events have faced growing threats of boycotts from voting rights advocates who say local corporations should have done more to oppose the legislation before it was signed into law. Coca-Cola and Delta sharply criticized the new legislation, so infuriating Republican leaders that there was a brief attempt to rescind a lucrative tax break that benefited the airline.

Some critics of the law have increasingly focused on the sporting industry, asking the NCAA and the World Cup to forgo Georgia for future premier events.

Baseball's All-Star game has been held in Atlanta twice — in 1972 at Atlanta Stadium (later renamed Atlanta-Fulton County Stadium) and in 2000 at Turner Field. ∎

ONLY A SPEEDBUMP

Chipper Jones Can Relate to Superstar Acuna's Season-Ending Injury

By Steve Hummer • July 12, 2021

Chipper Jones wasn't watching in real time when things got real bad for the Braves: Their young star Ronald Acuna crashing to earth with a blown-up knee in Miami.

But all news — especially the unsettling kind — spreads like a flame through the dry tinder of social media. And it wasn't long before Jones was messaging Braves GM Alex Anthopoulos with an offer to advise Acuna on what comes next.

Yes, please. For Jones is uniquely qualified to help and encourage here. He lived the same thing and came out the other side a Hall of Famer.

In fact, Jones was a year younger than the 23-year-old Acuna when his ACL popped as he twisted awkwardly trying to avoid a tag at first base during a spring training game in Fort Lauderdale, Fla., in 1994. And nowhere near as established as Acuna, at the time a 1990 No. 1 draft pick with all of four Major League plate appearances just playing his way onto the big club's roster.

"The first thing I will tell him," said Jones, "I will point right at that quad (the mass of muscle in his thigh) and say, 'Pay attention to that muscle right there.' "

And, after the practical rehab guidance, he'll want to add: " 'You are going to be fine. Yes, it sucks that you're going to miss a half of a year during the course of your career. I know you want to be out there for your teammates and your teammates want you out there. Hey, this is the reality. This is a speedbump. It's not going to derail your career in any shape or form. It is a speedbump.' "

What better example could Acuna draw from as he goes from the teary-eyed shock of the ligament tear to the arduous, unseen task of rehab from surgery? And so convenient, too, with Jones, the lifetime Brave, already on hand as a hitting consultant.

What faces Acuna is not going to be easy. "Twelve hours after they replace his ACL, they're going to bend his knee to a 90-degree angle. It's going to be one of the most painful things that he ever does in his life. But they have to get that range of motion back," Jones said.

It's not for the faint of heart. "Whenever you have a big knee injury — I'm not going to call it catastrophic, but it's every bit the Tommy John surgery of the knee — it's important to keep your confidence," Jones counseled.

It's not going to be in any way familiar for a young player who has always had a charmed and special relationship with every movement on the ballfield. "The game has always come easy to him. He was touched by God to play this game. He's unbelievable at it," Jones said. "Now, he's going to have to work to get his body back to where we all know that RAJ (as in Ronald Acuna Jr.) can be."

But the bottom line, Jones said, is that for all the short-term pain this injury has caused Acuna and the Braves, it does not have to be an ongoing obstacle. In fact, it could even serve him well in the future.

You could say it worked out OK for Jones after his surgery. He missed his chance to break in with the Braves in '94, but came back the next season to play in 140 games, hit .265 and 23 home runs for a World Series-winning team. The first of 18 seasons over which he switch-hit for 468 homers and 2,726 hits. Cooperstown was suitably impressed.

And yes, he could still run a little bit afterward. In Jones' MVP season of 1999, five years after the surgery, he stole

Braves right fielder Ronald Acuna Jr. attempts to walk after trying to make a catch on an inside-the-park home run hit by Miami Marlins' Jazz Chisholm Jr. Acuna was ruled out for the season with a torn ACL. (AP Images)

25 bases. But he doesn't recommend damaging the same knee at the age of 38, as he did. That will really slow down a person. Although even following that, Jones played two more seasons.

He recognizes now that his first knee injury was a sort of well-disguised blessing. It forced Jones to begin working on a neglected part of his body — his legs. Believing his swing was so much an upper-body experience, Jones before the injury had spent the majority of time working on his arms and shoulders.

"Now suddenly not only did I pay attention from my shoulders to my wrists, but I had to pay attention to my legs. I feel like it really helped me from a power and durability standpoint," he said.

"It really propelled me, especially when I grew up and kind of got my man-strength, being able to synch my swing with my legs and drive the ball to the opposite field," Jones said. "There's no doubt that injury and that rehab contributed to that."

Hence Jones' inclination to fixate on Acuna's quadriceps. Acuna will not lack for advice and motivational prodding. As Jones said, "If it's up to me, if it's up to anybody on the training staff, his family, I'm sure we'll all going to be pushing him because he's one of the most important players of our generation to come through this organization and we want to see him continue to develop and be the player we all know he can be." And for his part, Jones is likely to harp on the importance of building up those legs, immediately.

There is an upwelling of optimism to Jones' message. He comes bearing the belief that if Acuna gives his all to his rehab — and Jones has no reason to suspect he won't — all the great promise of the last three-plus seasons can't be denied.

"I'm telling you I would never wish an injury like this on anybody, but he could come back a bigger, better version of himself," Jones said.

He goes on: "He hits balls as far as I've ever seen anybody hit 'em. If he gets a big, strong lower half, he might be hitting balls 500 feet next year.

"There could be a little bit of something beneficial from this injury — at least that's the way I choose to look at it."

Precisely the type of aid and comfort so sorely needed now. ∎

Losing superstar Ronald Acuna Jr. was a devastating blow in the moment, but the Braves eventually adapted and acquired additional outfield depth to make up for the loss. (AP Images)

THIRD BASEMAN

27

AUSTIN RILEY

24-Year-Old Blossoms on Young, Loaded Infield

By Steve Hummer   August 15, 2021

Some science — when it's not life and death — needs denying. Like when a questioner mentioned to Brian Snitker that defensive metrics don't always treat his third baseman kindly.

Proud to say I know nothing of such numbers — and think even less of them. That they exist at all, I'll just have to take the word of those who care to turn the art of catching a baseball into an equation.

The Braves manager — bless him — agrees. Snitker's old-school was showing when he said in response to certain coefficients that libel Austin Riley's defense: "I don't pay any attention to defensive metrics. I judge defense by my eyes, not by numbers."

Snitker's eyes had just seen Riley dive full out to his right to backhand a line drive, spring to his feet and complete the put-out at first to save a Braves victory over Washington in August. Will Smith was in to close, so runners on base and high drama were inevitable. Riley saved the day with his glove.

As the Braves snack on the tapas and small plates that the schedule is now serving them, we should not let the quality of the competition diminish what they are accomplishing.

Their surge to the top of the NL East has been largely due to infield play that has bordered on the remarkable.

What we're witnessing now with this team's infield as a whole is a beautiful thing. In the absence of those bats belonging to Ronald Acuna and Marcell Ozuna, the Braves infielders have filled in with more than their share of production and power.

Everyone else — that includes you, Dodgers — put this between your cheek and gum and chaw on it: "That's as good an infield defensively and offensively as you'll see on any one team in the Major Leauges, in my opinion," Snitker said of his own.

Around the infield they all are bombing away and chipping in with such quantity it's difficult to focus on just one of them. But Riley's three hits and game-ending defensive play commanded the stage against the Nationals.

Watching the 24-year-old refine his approach at the plate, the flailing replaced by a reasoned eye, might be the greatest single pleasure in this show. Like the manager says, some things you just see and you know. And to see the light come on for Riley is to know that he no longer intends to be a pitcher's plaything.

"I'm happy for him, knowing (what he does) every day,

Austin Riley had a breakout season in 2021, hitting .303 with 33 HR and 107 RBI.
(Curtis Compton/The Atlanta Journal-Constitution)

watching this kid work and how consistent he is," Snitker said. "He comes to play every day. He's hung with himself as much as anything. That's the big key. These guys have to hang with themselves and believe in themselves — and he has."

"It's been a long process. Still a lot to learn. Still a lot to improve. But it's nice to help a ballclub," he said. Did we forget to mention he never comes off like a foghorn when talking about himself?

While it's difficult to strictly identify the 2021 MVP of the Braves because of all the infielders lining up for the title, Riley is right there. And if he is in the running for most valuable on a team chasing its fourth straight division title, then surely he must be a candidate for that honorific league-wide. Not that he can win it — he doesn't have the "brand" just yet. But Riley belongs in the conversation. No supporting data is necessary. Just watch him, you'll see it.

Above: Austin Riley reacts after hitting a walk-off RBI single in Game 1 of the NLCS against the Dodgers. (Hyosub Shin/The Atlanta Journal-Constitution) Opposite: Austin Riley had shown potential early in his career with the Braves, but his 2021 performance put him in the MVP conversation and announced him as one of the best young stars in the game. (Curtis Compton/The Atlanta Journal-Constitution)

BACK TO EVEN

Braves Finally Reach .500 After Slow Start to Season

By Mark Bradley • August 5, 2021

The Braves won consecutive games for the first time since Eddie Haas was deemed a managerial upgrade over Joe Torre. (Slight exaggeration, yes.) In four games since their July 30 deadline hires began to arrive, they're 3-1. (Small sample size, yes.) They remained 2½ games out of first place — also one game out of second — but let's be honest: They look a bit different.

Disclaimer: This is baseball, where looks often deceive, where momentum is tomorrow's starting pitcher, where the worst team can take three in a row from the best team. (Fun stat of the year: The mighty Dodgers are 1-10 in extra innings.) But it has been so long since the Braves have done much that the end of this goofy win/loss/win/loss/win/loss run of 18 games is worth noting, if not quite saluting.

With the absences of Ronald Acuna, Travis d'Arnaud and Marcell Ozuna, what should have been a potent lineup was reduced to half-strength. There wasn't so much a hole in the batting order as an abyss. The four infielders — Freeman, Albies, Swanson and Riley — were capable big-league hitters. That left five slots to be filled by players of replacement-level worth and the day's pitcher. Whenever Max Fried started, he became the Braves' fifth-best hitter.

(That's not an exaggeration. Fried has an offensive WAR rating of 0.5. Abraham Almonte is at 0.1. Cristian Pache was at minus-0.7. Kevan Smith is at minus-0.6.)

There are reasons Jorge Soler and Adam Duvall and Joc Pederson and Stephen Vogt were available for not very much in return. They're not superstars, though Soler hit 48 homers — while striking out 178 times — in 2019. But they're a cut above the journeymen the Braves had been forced to use as regulars.

It's hard for a good team, which we all expected this to be, to play 108 games without breaking .500, but here — as we know too well — this team sits. More honesty: Before Alex Anthopoulos made four deals on deadline day, I was close to giving up on this season. (And, having been around a while, I'm reluctant to say anything's over until it is. I'm an Atlantan. I witnessed 28-3.)

It wasn't so much that the Braves' general manager hooked one difference-maker as that he imported four guys — Eddie Rosario is on the injured list — who together might make a difference.

Example: Richard Rodriguez had been closing in Pittsburgh. In his first appearance as a Brave, Brian Snitker summoned him to work the fifth inning in a game the Braves trailed 3-2. You might think that's a low-leverage moment for a high-leverage guy, but how many times have we see the middle relief render a winnable game unwinnable?

Rodriguez faced Dylan Carlson, Paul Goldschmidt and Nolan Arenado, the Cardinals' two, three and four hitters. Against Drew Smyly in the first inning, they'd gone single, single, homer. Against Rodriguez, they went groundout, groundout, groundout. The Braves took the lead in the top of the sixth. Rodriguez as a Brave: three innings, 28 pitches, two hits, no walks, no earned runs.

The GM of a contender is supposed to make his team better at the deadline. Anthopoulos did. There's no guarantee that better will be good enough to catch and pass the Mets and Phillies over the final 54 games, but Philly doesn't scare anybody, and the Mets are without Jacob deGrom. Also, of the Braves' next 16 games, 13 will come against opponents below .500. This could, and maybe should, still happen. ∎

Outfielder Joc Pederson was one of several mid-season additions to the Braves roster that helped them gain momentum in the second half after a slow start to the season. (Curtis Compton/The Atlanta Journal-Constitution)

Once the Braves reached .500 in August, they never looked back on their way to a dominant regular season finish. (Hyosub Shin/The Atlanta Journal-Constitution)

SOAKING IN THE SUCCESS

An Old Coach and a Young Infield, the Perfect Combo

By Steve Hummer • August 19, 2021

The firm of Freeman, Albies, Swanson and Riley is now a leader in its field — the infield. And as it rises to eminence in the National League, so, too, it's fervently believed, will the Braves. It's kind of a package deal.

From his executive office — neither wood-paneled nor leather-upholstered; mostly grass, clay and spit — Ron Washington soaks in the success.

"That's what's most gratifying — the growth," the Braves third base/infield defense coach said, "seeing them from the first time I arrived here in Atlanta and seeing where they are today."

There's more. Washington never lacks for more to say: "They have grown tremendously, not only physically, but mentally. That's the joy, when the game starts, to sit back and watch 'em play. They make mistakes like anybody else, but I tell you what, they get after it. They believe in defense. It's a part of them. It's so much a part of them. That's what you try to build, and that's the joy I get just watching them play."

It is one of the great cross-generational partnerships in baseball. A still young infield — only first baseman Freddie Freeman is on the other side of 30, with second baseman Ozzie Albies, shortstop Dansby Swanson and Austin Riley at third averaging out at 25 years old — and the 69-year-old coach who has connected with them in a joyful, productive, almost familial way.

Their bond is built upon the daily ritual of brief, concentrated fielding drills of Washington's invention.

Individually, each player pops out pregame to a patch of foul-ground grass, where "Wash," as he's known in these quarters, feeds him about 100 ground balls, some by hand, some off the narrow barrel of his surgical fungo bat. Using a variety of gloves ranging from what looks like a small, round throw pillow to their game-day leather, taking hops from their knees and while on their feet, each infielder builds upon various skills. Refining hand-eye coordination. Catching the ball in the palm of the glove rather than the webbing. Pairing athletic ability with proper positioning and the best angles from which to wrangle a bounding hardball. Growing closer around the pursuit of a shared goal.

"There is no perfection in baseball," the shaman of infield play said. "Sometimes the ball is going to beat us. But the majority of the time we're going to beat the ball before it has a chance to beat us. That's what that's about on the side every single day."

Two traits define these drills.

First, the running commentary/banter supplied by the chatty Washington, rated as it is a hard R. "He is one of those baseball guys you can't bring your kids around, but it's just fun," Freeman said as he chuckled. "He goes at it with Ozzie all day long — one thing after another."

Secondly, there's the devotion the players show them. This is the secular baseball version of daily Mass.

The drills aren't mandatory. "I'll be at a spot from 2 o'clock to 4:30, or in the mornings during spring training, I'm there from 7:30 to 9:30. If they want something, come

Second baseman Ozzie Albies shows off the glove work he's developed over the years with third base/infield coach Ron Washington. (Hyosub Shin/The Atlanta Journal-Constitution)

get it. If they don't come, I'm not upset," Washington said. "Someone is going to show up, and that someone who shows up, if he's coming to get something, he's going to get it, and everybody else is going to see it and everybody is going to want some of it."

No day goes by with Washington idle. A guy may take a pass here or there over the season's long haul. Although he can't recall the last session missed by Freeman or Albies, with whom Washington formed a particularly strong bond when he began with the Braves in 2017 and the then-prospect was coming back from a fractured elbow with little else to do but drill.

What would seem to be the height of monotony has become a trademark of an infield that is coming together like a sturdy brick wall. With Washington as the mason.

"It can get repetitive," Freeman said. "There are day games where you think, 'Aw, I can take a day off.' But you don't want to because it's actually fun, and you've made it a part of your routine. When you have a guy who is almost 70 who brings that kind of energy every single day — who is working pretty much as hard as we are on a daily basis, well, it's just amazing what he does and what he means to us."

At the plate, what this Braves infield is doing now hardly meshes with Washington's experience. All four have more home runs thus far this season than Washington hit over parts of 10 seasons as a utility infielder with five teams through the 1980s (20). He'll tell you there's a good reason for this: Players are bigger and stronger, and pitching is watered down. "That's just my opinion," he said. And he'll run out of opinions when Vidalia runs out of onions.

From the confines of his third-base box, it's Washington's job to keep waving Braves base runners home. Defensively is where he has a more personal connection to his guys. And when any of them make a play like Riley did to secure a one-run win over Washington — a diving, game-ending stab of a ground ball up the line — Washington shares in a healthy slice of satisfaction. "What makes me so proud of every one of those guys is how they apply the things they work on every single day," he said.

The secret to the relationships he has built? Pay attention CEOs, you might learn something.

"Listening and learning, those are the two qualities any teacher/coach has to have," he said.

Third baseman Austin Riley and third base coach Ron Washington get in some work before Game 3 of the NLCS. (Curtis Compton/The Atlanta Journal-Constitution)

"You have to listen. And when you're learning, it's not just one way, it's two ways. The only way you can know what they need and be able to give it to them all the time is to listen to what they're talking about. And when you listen, you learn about the people. Then as a coach, you know how to approach them."

Furthermore, "Players want to be led. They want to be responsible. You make them responsible by not forcing them to do things but letting them know the availability is there. There is some wisdom, some knowledge, some experience, some growth — all of that is available if you want to come get it."

There is something of Washington that has rubbed off on this unit. Yes, there are all his mechanics and theories for catching a ball. But also, there's the constancy of his love for the game and the ageless service he has given it.

God knows Washington has had his trials. His imperfections have been run up the flagpole more than once. As the only manager who has taken the Texas Rangers to the World Series (in 2010 and '11), he tested positive for cocaine in 2010. He worked through that only to abruptly resign the job in 2014 to repair a marriage damaged by his infidelity, he said.

His disappointment in not being able to get another managing job remains to this day. "I have no doubt that if the opportunity presents itself, I can lead a club where it needs to go. I have no doubt about that,"

Ron Washington has played many roles over the years in MLB, but his energy and willingness to engage with players on their terms has remained consistent. (Curtis Compton/The Atlanta Journal-Constitution)

Washington said last week.

Yet he never hesitated to take lesser jobs after leaving Texas, first with Oakland and then with the Braves. He couldn't imagine not sharing himself with the next-generation ballplayer. Even now, with a 70th birthday tottering just ahead of him, he can't see a day when he's not out leading a drill.

"My body aches just like any 69-year-old guy's body aches," he said. "But I have a purpose every day. My purpose is to come to the ballpark for a game I dearly love. I never stopped loving the game of baseball. I'm on this earth right now — just like the guys who preceded me and taught me — to make a difference and try to help."

"Right now, my mind is still working. As far as my body goes, my body does what I tell it to," Washington said.

The coach continues to coach himself up, too — ultimately some of his best work yet. ∎

RIGHT FIELDER

14

ADAM DUVALL

Midseason Acquisition Overcomes All — and Braves are Lucky He Has

By Steve Hummer   September 16, 2021

Those watching Adam Duvall and his Braves Just Can't Live Without Me Comeback Tour don't see it. Who could know as the home runs and RBI continued to build up about all the days when he just doesn't feel exactly right? Those days when he's riding the blood-sugar elevator and can't quite get to the floor he wants. Because Duvall will never show it.

Sure, the insulin pump that discreetly tags along in the back pocket of his baseball britches has been a godsend. He has the best medical and nutritional support available. Still, playing major league ball — more than that, standing as one of the most productive power hitters in the game — while dealing with Type 1 diabetes isn't nearly as easy as Duvall makes it look.

Every other body out there on the field naturally is doing the work of regulating the glucose that fuels every play. The diabetic has lost that luxury, and needs help striking a tricky, elusive balance.

Nothing to do but live with the inevitable spikes and dips.

"When I go low (in blood sugar), I start to get jitters," Duvall said.

"When I go high, I'll be very tired and sluggish."

And just how many days in a long season does Duvall figure that he's just a little off, one way or another?

"I would say half of the days probably," he estimated. You would never know it.

"You're dealing with a disease every day. There is still a lot of manual work that goes into it," he explained.

There's the humbling route taken to get here. The Braves first traded for a one-time All Star in mid-2018, only to use Duvall sparingly and send him packing to Triple-A Gwinnett to start the next season after hitting only .132 with no homers in 53 at-bats.

Did he big-time it and pout as a Striper? No, he quietly applied himself there and hit bombs from Memphis to Norfolk to Durham (32 of them in 101 games) until the Braves had no choice but to bring him back for the close of 2019 and the COVID-shortened 2020. There he provided much of the punch that had been missing (26 home runs, 52 RBI in 74 games total).

Only to be non-tendered by the Braves at the end of last season, opening the door to free agency and Duvall's relocation to Miami and the Marlins. But when the Braves' outfield was depleted by injury (Ronald Acuna) and domestic strife (Marcell Ozuna) and their lineup lost all that muscle, who, among a few others, did they turn back to? The Braves just might be coming around to the notion that Duvall is good for them — slowly — like he's kale or flossing.

For the price of a young, unproven catcher, they got the 33-year-old back at the end of July and he has been nothing but a run producer since.

When the Braves reacquired him, the benefit went two ways — not only did they get back his bat, but now he also could no longer use it to kneecap them.

Adam Duvall not only thrived in his return to the Braves during the 2021 season, but did it while dealing with Type 1 diabetes. (Curtis Compton/The Atlanta Journal-Constitution)

"He just torched us when he was with the Marlins," Braves manager Brian Snitker said. "I was so happy when we could get him back and get him out of Miami and get him with us." In a dozen games against the Braves this year, Duvall hit .368 with five homers and 17 RBIs.

But to truly appreciate Duvall's wending journey, you need to take all of the resilience he has shown in the last three years and add to it the difficulties of playing a hard game at an elite level while managing diabetes.

His accepting, patient attitude about it all is reflected in his walk-up music at Truist Park: "Call Me the Breeze."

Duvall could be a little smug now if he chose to be, given how the Braves had to use a Mulligan to get him back after once demoting him and then non-tendering him. But he makes a wiser choice.

"God put me where I needed to be, and that was that. Was I excited to come back? Yeah, because this is a cool, special place for me," he said.

Expanding on special, Duvall added, "It's where I spent the last three and a half years. A lot of good memories. A lot of ups and downs. There have been some tough times, but when you get through those tough times and come back through, that's what makes it special.

"That's the journey, that's what makes it special, the ups and downs, coming out on the other side of it. Life or sports or anything is not always going to be easy. I'm a true believer in how you deal with things, and I chose to not deal with it in a personal way. When they sent me down to Gwinnett was that where I wanted to be — absolutely not. But I felt I went down there and did what I needed to do to get back up, and I feel like I've made the most of it."

So happy were the Braves to have him back that Snitker rushed him into the lineup the day of the trade, admitting later he probably overtaxed Duvall at the time. Otherwise, his diabetes is no issue when making out the lineup card. Currently playing in center, he has the durability and defensive chops to anchor the Braves outfield.

Duvall's trademark isn't hitting for average as a career .232 hitter. But he ranked among National League leaders in hitting with runners in scoring position, his stock in trade is timely pop.

Instead, here's his approach: "It's not just runners in scoring position — if you can drive runners in from first or drive yourself in from home, you're going to help yourself out in the RBI situation. It's kind of a joke, but the mentality is that

Adam Duvall was a big-time run producer in 2021, knocking in 113 runs for the season, including 45 in just 55 games for the Braves. (Curtis Compton/The Atlanta Journal-Constitution)

every time I hit, I've got somebody in scoring position — that's myself. I have the ability to drive myself in. That's the mentality when I go up there."

You don't see the small insulin pump that levels out the symptoms of the diabetes that was diagnosed relatively late, when he was 23, playing high Single-A ball. You don't know of those weary nights when he gets into town to start a road series, when he just wants to fall into bed, but first his schedule demands he find a new spot to stick himself and move his pump site before he can sleep. You don't need to know that.

But Duvall wants people to know that with the right approach, look what's possible.

"I try to have a good attitude and good outlook on (his diabetes). I would never try to disguise it because I want kids to know that you can play a sport (with it). If you put the time and effort and commitment into handling it the way you should, I feel like you basically can do anything you want to do."

Just as he told a youngster in Washington earlier this season, the one he met following the game after noticing the sign he waved at Duvall proclaiming that he was a diabetic, too. There are 1.6 million people with Type 1 diabetes in the U.S. according to the American Diabetes Association. But precious few in baseball (injured St. Louis pitcher Jordan Hicks is one other).

Once, Duvall said, "I kinda lived and died by my at-bats or my performance." Experience, marriage, fatherhood has lent him a healthier perspective. He sees himself as a polar opposite of who he was just 10 years ago.

So, when asked about where he sees himself next season — he and the Braves have a mutual option for 2022, although the team may well rework a deal — all he says, Zen-like, is, "Just be where your feet are."

And when outlining the priorities for himself as a player, he doesn't need you to know the challenges he faces, just the consistency he tries for in spite of them.

"For me, it's important to come in here and be a good teammate because that's never really looked at from a fans' standpoint," Duvall said. "It's come in here, help your teammates get better, which in turn is going to 100 percent help you get better. And come out and win ballgames. How I help them win ballgames is driving runners in and playing good defense. That's what I come to park each and every day trying to do."

Adam Duvall, acquired by the Braves at the end of July, was a big part of the team's success in the second half of the season. (Curtis Compton/The Atlanta Journal-Constitution)

SECOND BASEMAN

1

OZZIE ALBIES

Young Star Makes Braves History with 30 Home Run, 100 RBI Season

By Gabriel Burns September 23, 2021

Ozzie Albies is rapidly becoming one of the best power-hitting second basemen in MLB history. Albies reached the 30 home run, 100 RBI plateau during the 2021 season, finishing the season with 30 homers and 106 runs batted in. Albies reached the 30-100 mark at 24 years and 258 days old, becoming the youngest second baseman in MLB history to reach the mark.

He's the fourth second baseman with a 30 homer, 100 RBI season since 2010, joining Dan Uggla (2010), Robinson Cano (2016) and Jonathan Scoop (2017).

"What an accomplishment," manager Brian Snitker said of Albies' season. "In the storied history of the Atlanta Braves, to be the first guy to do that is pretty cool. That's really neat. He's just a little fella, you know? I'm happy for Oz. ... Ozzie is that boring pro, just the same thing every day. I never see that guy have a bad day. His attitude, it's off the charts. It's unbelievable. He's such a cool young man."

The switch-hitter is the third Braves second baseman to hit 30 home runs in a season, joining Davey Johnson (43 in 1973) and Uggla (36 in 2011). He's the first primary middle infielder in franchise history to post a 100 RBI season. His 90 career homers already are the franchise record for second basemen.

The Braves' infield as a whole was potent in 2021. Third baseman Austin Riley had 33 homers, 2020 National League most valuable player Freddie Freeman had 31 and Albies had 30. Shortstop Dansby Swanson had 27 home runs, placing the team within three home runs of becoming the first infield in MLB history in which each starting member had 30 home runs.

Albies said the infield is "no doubt" the best in MLB.

"I don't see how anybody else can compete with it," said starter Ian Anderson, agreeing that the Braves' infield is baseball's best. "The defense speaks for itself, coming from the pitching side of things. Obviously to hit for the power they have, to drive in runs and get on base as they have, it's been awesome to watch."

A constant source of energy and positivity for the Braves, the 24-year-old Ozzie Albies is on a trajectory to be one of the best players in franchise history. (Curtis Compton/The Atlanta Journal-Constitution)

Braves second baseman Ozzie Albies reacts to a single against the Milwaukee Brewers in the sixth inning of Game 4 of the NLDS. (Curtis Compton/The Atlanta Journal-Constitution)

BUILDING ON THE FLY

How the Braves GM Made His Outfield Makeover Work

By Steve Hummer • October 1, 2021

The human puzzle that is a baseball clubhouse is the most complicated kind. Imagine a jigsaw puzzle where the pieces change shape day to day according to mood or fortune. How do you ever put together anything that produces a pleasing, or even coherent, picture? Let alone rebuild it after some of the pieces get lost in the green shag carpet.

Braves general manager Alex Anthopoulos tries to simplify the puzzle by reducing the pieces. Take the pool of players who possess the requisite talent and shrink it to more manageable size, he said, to include "those players who fit what you're trying to do."

And when you do that right, then just maybe it is possible to rebuild an outfield on the fly and turn a season that seemed doomed into the fourth in a series of National League East championships.

The oft-told wonder of this Braves division title was how they replaced an entire outfield late, touching off an almost instant chemical reaction that changed everything.

Your Braves outfield July 16, the first game back from the All-Star break, the team 4½ games out of first: Abraham Almonte in right; Guillermo Heredia in center; Orlando Arcia in left. Star outfielder Ronald Acuna had been lost to a knee injury and 2020's Silver Slugger Award winner as a DH, Marcell Ozuna, was entangled in a domestic-violence issue.

The outfield for your division champion Braves on clinch day, Sept. 30: Jorge Soler in right; Adam Duvall in center; Eddie Rosario in left. All three acquired at the trade deadline, July 30. All three credited with helping ignite a nine-game road win streak late in the season. All three representing some of Anthopoulos' finest work.

"The guts of this lineup came the first of August," first baseman Freddie Freeman said. "It made a huge difference. It made a huge difference in our lineup, made a huge difference in the makeup of our team and how our team felt about itself.

"We had a lot of injuries. We needed players and (Anthopoulos) went out and got four major league outfielders (including Joc Pederson in mid-July). And every one of them came in and made an immediate impact which was awesome."

Or, as second baseman Ozzie Albies put it, "We needed big bats at big moments and they showed up."

Anthopoulos was trying anything to kickstart a team that spent its first 110 games never seeing the sunny side of .500. At Freeman's urgings and against his own fears of fostering a fatter roster, he had a soft-serve ice cream installed in the clubhouse. And then told Freeman that if the Braves won the NL East, he'd have one delivered to his home. Freeman hasn't pushed that point yet. "I owe him. If he ever wants to call me on it, it will be money well spent," Anthopoulos said.

More substantive were the moves made to plug the holes in the Braves outfield dike.

It's not like Anthopoulos picked up a used Yugo and won the Daytona 500 or took best-in-show at Westminster with a rescue mutt. He was trading in more known quantities than that, in players who were accomplished but in many cases were underproducing or hurt or both. (That, in turn, made them more affordable). Still, what the Braves GM did this season with his trade deadline maneuverings — turning low-cost acquisitions into treasure — has smacked of the unbelievable.

Acquired at the trade deadline alongside fellow outfielders Adam Duvall and Eddie Rosario, Jorge Soler provided a major boost to the injury-laden Braves lineup. (Curtis Compton/The Atlanta Journal-Constitution)

Besides adding a bit of payroll burden to a corporation that can take it, Anthopoulos acquired these difference-making players without giving up a top-15 prospect. The Braves were desperate, yet none of the deals emitted the burnt-hair aroma of desperation.

There is no guarantee, of course, that such mid-season transplants won't be rejected. Yet what marked the Braves trades was how all four outfielders quickly integrated into their new surroundings and flourished. Some dramatically so. Soler, who hit 48 homers in Kansas City in 2019, was hitting just .192 and slugging just .370 in 94 games with the Royals before the trade.

Here's where Anthopoulos' beliefs in scouting personality as well as performance paid off. Into a clubhouse already designed around certain high expectations came another group of players pre-wired to work on the same current.

"Alex looks for good people first. That's huge in a clubhouse," said Duvall, on his second go-round with the Braves. "When you can get all the guys gelling and meshing and playing together it's different than a bunch of guys playing for themselves. That's what he looks for and that's what he brings in. That's big for a team in a spot we were in earlier; we needed to make up some ground. Then, you can't bring in guys who aren't going to fit in right away."

Soler is a study in how organizationally the Braves can make a new piece fit. His manager had faith in him — sensing Soler was ready to break out, Brian Snitker plugged him into the lineup one day earlier than originally planned. His outfield coach had faith in him — Eric Young assured all that Soler, who was DHing the bulk of the time in K.C., would be a more than competent outfielder. And his teammates were eager to bring out his best.

"I consider myself a pretty timid person," Soler said through an interpreter. "When I first got here, I was very quiet, not really talking to anyone. Thank God, I had (Heredia) here with me, another Cuban. He was able to introduce me to the guys and make me feel welcome. Once that started getting going, I was able to make friends with everybody."

"Some places you can put too many mismatched parts together and it's not easy. The core group here and the makeup of this club makes it such that it's an easy environment to come in and feel you want to be a part of it," Snitker said.

Then, of course, if you can't get cranked up leaving a non-contender for a team in the grips of a division race, Anthopoulos probably wouldn't be pursuing you.

"It's a very special moment for me and my family. I didn't start the season very well, but I had the blessing to come to this team and here we are," Soler said during the division-clinching celebration.

The story of this division championship, as much as the MVP-caliber rise of Austin Riley and the performance of two front-line starters — Charlie Morton and Max Fried — has been the rescue effort of Anthopoulos in the face of potentially crippling losses and the work of an emergency outfield.

"I'll be the first to say you have your doubts," Freeman said, "but then they come in and you start winning."

"I don't want to do this again. I never want to experience something like this again. Definitely, the most challenging year, for sure," Anthopoulos said.

Hand in hand with that, he added, "Under the circumstances of all we went through I'd say it is the most rewarding year of my career." ∎

Eddie Rosario celebrates in the Braves dugout after scoring during Game 1 of the NLCS. (Hyosub Shin/The Atlanta Journal-Constitution)

THE BEST YET

Braves Win Fourth Straight NL East Title; This One Might Be Most Impressive

By Gabriel Burns • September 30, 2021

The last three divisional triumphs, unique in their own ways, might not compare to the Braves' path in 2021.

In 2018, the upstart Braves were a feel-good story. It was an organization that emerged from a complete teardown (and embarrassing controversy) to win a division. A year later, the Braves cemented themselves as a 97-win power, again claiming the NL East before seeing their season go down in flames with a disastrous Game 5 loss at home to the Cardinals in the NL Division Series.

In 2020, there were legitimate questions as to whether there'd be an MLB season due to the coronavirus pandemic. The Braves wound up 35-25 in the shortened campaign, winning two series in the expanded postseason and earning their first NL Championship Series berth in nearly two decades.

While the Braves fell short against the eventual champion Dodgers, they held their heads high. They retained the core of their roster and expected to be right back in the mix in 2021.

This path featured multiple detours, bumps in the road and a few scares of veering off course. Through it all, the result was the same: The Braves are National League East champions for the fourth consecutive year, secured with a late September win over the Phillies at Truist Park.

"Not to take anything away from those other teams, but this is by far the most special title," general manager Alex Anthopoulos said during the Braves' champagne-soaked celebration.

The Braves faced adversity over the past three years, but none could equal what they endured this time. The Braves were mired in misfortune, bad luck, injuries, self-inflicted wounds and statistical anomalies. It wasn't until Aug. 6 that they achieved a winning record — they joined the lowly Marlins and Rangers as the only teams to never hold a winning mark until finally breaking through.

"I'm just so proud of these guys," manager Brian Snitker said. "Where we came from, the different lineup changes, just hanging in there. To pull this thing off is unbelievable. Everything we went through, the injuries we had to overcome. Everybody has injuries, but we had some huge injuries with our team. Credit to Alex and his team for what they did at the deadline. It's a really gratifying feeling."

Listing the Braves' misfortunes is a time-consuming endeavor. Some of the lowlights: Young All-Star starter Mike Soroka was first expected back in late April — he never pitched, as his final setback was re-tearing the Achilles that also ended his 2020 campaign. Outfielder Marcell Ozuna, re-signed after starring on a one-year deal, broke his fingers and then was arrested for domestic violence in May.

Catcher Travis d'Arnaud, a Silver Slugger last season, tore a ligament in his thumb that sidelined him for months. Opening-day center fielder Cristian Pache wasn't ready for the majors, leading to a demotion. Shane Greene, signed to help stabilize the bullpen, was ineffective and dropped in August.

The Braves nonetheless treaded water earlier in the summer. They were 30-35, sitting eight games out, June 16. They closed the gap to four games by the All-Star break, but it wasn't without cost: Superstar outfielder Ronald Acuna tore his ACL one day before the break.

With their MVP candidate gone, so seemed the Braves' chances. Making matters worse, promising young starter

Relievers A.J. Minter (left) and Luke Jackson soak in the moment after the Braves clinched their fourth straight National League East title. (Hyosub Shin/The Atlanta Journal-Constitution)

73

Ian Anderson had shoulder discomfort and would be evaluated over the break. The Braves felt like a house of cards collapsing. To outside observers, they were a cross-off. The first-place Mets, behind the momentum of new ownership, seemed ticketed for the postseason.

"When you lose the guys we lost, everyone has doubts," first baseman Freddie Freeman admitted. "Things were piling on at the All-Star break."

The Braves had an uphill climb even before Acuna's injury. They hadn't crossed .500 all year. Their lineup was a shell of its 2020 version. The team's only hope was its division's mediocrity, which kept the team within striking distance despite a season of Murphy's Law.

Then came the 2021 trade deadline, which will be remembered as one of the most important in franchise history. The transactions started early, with Anthopoulos acquiring outfielder Joc Pederson from the Cubs and catcher Stephen Vogt from Arizona before the second half opened.

Anthopoulos later explained how important the timing of those moves was. He didn't want the clubhouse to lose its inspiration with Acuna down.

"I was very concerned with what the mindset of the players was going to be during the break and coming out of the break," Anthopoulos told The AJC. "The timing of the Pederson and the Vogt deals was important in my mind, just to show the (incumbent) players. We had an important stretch after the break, too. … We didn't want the conversation coming out of the break to be, 'They've lost Anderson. They've lost Acuna. Are they just going to start trading players away?' That wasn't the case.

"The timing of the Pederson and Vogt deals … we tried to accelerate those, tried to have them done right when we got back, as much for the mindset of the players and coaches. We were going to continue to push forward and try to win."

Winning didn't happen immediately. What followed was perfected mediocrity: Excluding a suspended game against the Padres that was finished last week, the Braves opened the second half by alternating 18 consecutive wins and losses. And while the record won't stand because the suspended game's result is backdated, it beautifully illustrated the Braves' maddening, yet consistent, inconsistency.

On July 30, Anthopoulos refused to wave the white flag. He made four other trades, adding outfielders Jorge Soler,

The Braves' 2021 regular season was beset by injuries and subsequent roster shuffling, but the team rallied together to go the distance. (Hyosub Shin/The Atlanta Journal-Constitution)

Adam Duvall and Eddie Rosario, along with reliever Richard Rodriguez. The Braves dropped two of three to the Brewers that weekend before their season transformed.

The 18-game streak of mediocrity ended in early August, when the Braves swept then-struggling St. Louis on the road to reach .500. They defeated the Nationals in their first game back home to earn a winning record for the first time this season (56-55).

What followed was the turning point. The Braves (59-57), then 1½ games back, embarked on a nine-game road trip against three horrific teams, the Nationals, Marlins and Orioles. They swept the three-city trip, taking sole possession of first place in the middle of their run and returning home with a 68-57 record.

Just like that, a season of disappointment turned into hope, perhaps even expectation, that the Braves would again make the postseason. They've had highs and lows since their road surge, but that sequence proved the difference maker in their season.

"That was huge because in baseball, you can look back and say, 'Oh, you're supposed to win against those teams,' but you never know," Freeman said. "The game of baseball is crazy. When you take care of business, it built our confidence going forward that we expected to win. We have a really good team."

It's a story of perseverance. A group of newcomers arrived and meshed — a testament to the Braves' infrastructure, while the incumbents excelled. Third baseman Austin Riley, who received a healthy share of "MVP" chants at Truist Park, has been a star. Starters Max Fried and Charlie Morton have been brilliant, giving this team an advantage those before it couldn't claim: dual aces atop the rotation. The once-thin lineup is stacked with power.

"I think you can stack our team up against anyone," Freeman said. "You have to run through Charlie Morton, Max Fried, Ian Anderson, I like our chances. Our offense can put some runs on the board. I feel really confident going forward."

"I've never been part of a season that had as much adversity as this one had," shortstop Dansby Swanson said. "But I feel like that's a good characteristic for this team, to battle and fight for everything. I feel like we've earned every bit of what we have this year. That's a good thing going into the postseason." ■

Braves players celebrate their division title in the fountain at Truist Park after a win against the Philadelphia Phillies. (Hyosub Shin/The Atlanta Journal-Constitution)

LEFT FIELDER

8

EDDIE ROSARIO

The Mystery Man Who Bolstered the Braves

By Gabriel Burns · September 30, 2021

Left fielder Eddie Rosario was an overlooked name during the Braves' flurry of moves July 30. The team acquired him for a fading Pablo Sandoval in what amounted to a salary dump for the small-market Indians. Making the trade even less noteworthy was Rosario's abdominal injury, which meant he was weeks away from playing. The Braves sold the trade essentially as "additional depth."

Further muting any conversation around Rosario was his Triple-A production. He hit .196/.226/.471 with Gwinnett, although he finished on a 9-for-31 run before rejoining the club. There were no expectations as to what he could provide. The other acquisitions already were showing their worth and getting anything out of Rosario would've been a bonus.

It turns out, in a series of brilliant moves by general manager Alex Anthopoulos, none might have provided more bang-for-buck value than Rosario, considering he was added at no cost outside a pinch of payroll flexibility.

At the end of September, Rosario was hitting .272/.341/.580 with three doubles, two triples, six homers and 14 RBIs over 29 games. That's an uptick from his numbers in Cleveland, where hit .254 with 15 doubles, seven homers and 46 RBIs across 78 games before his injury.

"He's been huge for us," said outfielder Adam Duvall, another deadline acquisition who's helped make the Braves a postseason contender.

Rosario, 29, has made 25 starts in left field since he was activated from the injured list Aug. 27. He's been more important for the reimagined Braves outfield than expected. Less than a full season removed from a 32-homer campaign, Rosario has looked every bit as potent as he did in 2019. He's another reason the Braves' lineup is laden with pop.

And he's been clutch: He became the eighth player in Braves history to hit for the cycle during his team's series finale in San Francisco, helping the Braves avoid a sweep. It was the fourth contest of a hot five-game stretch in which Rosario hit .556 (10-for-18) with five extra-base hits, including three homers, and four RBIs.

"I'm really happy for him," starter Max Fried said after Rosario's cycle. "His first cycle in a big spot. We really needed that. It's really cool. Getting multiple hits is hard, let alone four and one of each."

Later in the western trip, Rosario produced the game-tying bloop hit in the ninth inning of Saturday's wild win over the Padres, which might be looked back upon as the most thrilling victory of the season.

Quietly added to the roster at the trade deadline, Eddie Rosario made his presence felt deep into the postseason. (Curtis Compton/The Atlanta Journal-Constitution)

"I think he's one of the best hitters out there," said Jorge Soler, who saw Rosario plenty when both played in the American League Central. "I feel like any time you see him with a runner in scoring position, I have 100 percent certainty that he was going to drive him in. That was truly an amazing at-bat against one of the best closers in the league (Mark Melancon). I can't say enough about him."

In the Braves' most important win to date, Rosario had an RBI double in their 7-2 win over the Phillies, which put them on the doorstep of earning their fourth consecutive division crown. The Braves wouldn't be here without Rosario and the other July newcomers.

Anthopoulos' trade deadline will be discussed as a notable point in recent Braves history. Rather than wave the white flag, he swung six trades that altered his team's fortunes in the uninspiring National League East.

Rosario, who seemed nothing more than a cheap flier at the time, has proved valuable beyond any expectation. He's been a vital role player in the Braves' pennant chase. He's also bolstered his own value as he prepares to re-enter the free-agent market this winter. Common sense says the Braves will be among the interested parties.

For now, everyone's focus lies on the Braves officially securing their spot in the playoffs, which could be just hours away. If that happens, Rosario will have the chance to further better his 2021 resume with postseason production.

Eddie Rosario celebrates with outfielders Guillermo Heredia and Adam Duvall after beating the Dodgers in Game 4 of the NLCS. (Curtis Compton/The Atlanta Journal-Constitution)

THE ODD COUPLE

A Forced Marriage Between Manager and GM Grows Into Beautiful Partnership

By Mark Bradley • October 6, 2021

They've won four division titles over four years. They've worked together in the way John Schuerholz did with Bobby Cox. One guy got the players; the other stitched together a first-place club every doggone year.

When Schuerholz arrived from Kansas City, the new general manager didn't get to hire his manager, Cox having been GM before team president Stan Kasten convinced him to return to the dugout in June 1990. Alex Anthopoulos likewise inherited Brian Snitker. Therein hangs a tale.

Snitker became the Braves' manager May 17, 2016. He'd been summoned from Gwinnett, where he was managing the Triple-A club. He flew to Pittsburgh, where the Braves had lost to fall to 9-28 under Fredi Gonzalez, who had seen nearly all his good players sold in the rebuild launched by president John Hart and GM John Coppolella.

Snitker has worked in the Braves' organization since 1977. He was signed as a player, which didn't last long. By 1982, he was managing the Anderson Braves in the Sally League. He became the classic company man, willing to go anywhere and do anything. He coached third base for Cox and Gonzalez. He managed Jeff Francoeur and Paul Byrd at Greenville. At 60, Snitker was still prepping minor-leaguers for their shot at the bigs.

Hart and Coppolella fired Gonzalez because the manager who led the Braves to the playoffs in 2012 and 2013 wasn't fully invested in the concept of losing on purpose. (Managers never are. All those L's go by their names.) The two Johns saw Snitker as a caretaker — he wouldn't make anything worse, and he might make it a bit better. He wasn't promised to keep his new job beyond the 2016 season.

It was assumed that the Johns would thank Snitker for his service and hire Bud Black, who was between jobs. (Black had been a pitcher. The Braves were rebuilding around pitching. 2+2=4.) On the morning of the final game at Turner Field, Hart floated the notion of a one-year extension for Snitker. The Braves entered September at 50-83. They went 18-10 thereafter. Julio Teheran beat Justin Verlander 1-0 in the team's sign-off to downtown.

Hart felt Snitker deserved a reward for keeping his players interested — whenever asked, they'd say they loved the guy — but the front office wasn't ready to make a long-term commitment. Snitker was offered another year, which was almost an insult. Having no other jobs lined up and not ready to retire, he took it.

The 2017 season was weird. The Braves opened SunTrust Park, now Truist Park. They shouldn't have been very good, but they were 45-45 two weeks before the trade deadline. Snitker, believing his best chance to keep managing was to win even if upper management still expected him to lose, was trying everything.

When Freddie Freeman returned from a broken wrist July 4, he did so as a third baseman. Matt Adams had hit a ton while serving as Freeman's stand-in, and Snitker wanted to get both bats in the lineup. That lasted 16 games.

General Manager Alex Anthopoulos and manager Brian Snitker embrace after the Braves clinched the National League pennant. (Curtis Compton/The Atlanta Journal-Constitution)

Dansby Swanson, the centerpiece of Coppolella's greatest trade, had become the face of the franchise after a promising 2016 debut, but he was demoted to Gwinnett to clear a spot for Johan Camargo. The front office couldn't grasp why Snitker gave journeyman Adonis Garcia so many starts at third base while Rio Ruiz, then considered a prospect of worth, sat idle.

On the next-to-last Saturday of the 2017 season, Snitker asked to meet with Hart/Coppolella early at the ballpark. Relations between the field manager and the men upstairs had frayed. A few weeks earlier, Hart stormed into the manager's office to upbraid him for allowing Jim Johnson to blow a ninth-inning lead against Seattle. (Despite the Braves' commitment to losing, Hart still took losses hard.)

Snitker figured he was about to get fired — full disclosure: this correspondent advocated such a move — but he had points he wanted to make. He made them so well that the meeting ended with Hart leaning toward giving Snitker yet another year, even though Black was still available. Everyone who meets the man says so, but that makes it no less true: It is impossible not to like Brian Snitker.

On the Monday after the season ended, MLB announced it was investigating the Braves for improprieties in the international talent market. Coppolella resigned that day. Amid the coast-to-coast embarrassment, Snitker's status became a footnote. A week before MLB slapped the Braves with heavy sanctions — Coppolella was banned for life; Hart announced he was stepping down the next day — the Braves introduced Anthopoulos as GM. Snitker greeted him at the press conference. It was the first time the men had met.

We had no way of knowing it then, but chaos left the Braves with an ideal one-two punch. Anthopoulos proved himself as Toronto's GM, and he proved he had standards by resigning — this after leading the Blue Jays to the 2015 AL East title — because he was uncomfortable with a rearranged front office. He spent two seasons as assistant GM under Andrew Friedman with the Dodgers, a time Anthopoulos saw as "grad school."

Anthopoulos is a great talker without being a big talker. He inherited the top-ranked farm system that Coppolella assembled and felt no urge to tear it up just because it wasn't of his making. He didn't bat an eye at the Braves' corporate ownership, having worked under the corporation Rogers Communications with Toronto. He made small moves trying to deepen the roster, a lesson he learned in L.A., and he could back away from a big move — a long-term contract for the 34-year-old Josh Donaldson, say — if it didn't make financial sense.

Anthopoulos gets the players; Snitker puts them to work. A forced marriage has grown into a beautiful partnership. That this team kept fighting when the fight seemed lost had much to do with Snitker. The Braves of old couldn't bear to let Cox down; the same applies to this manager and these men. That the Braves tore through August and September was a function of Anthopoulos' many deadline buys.

The two don't have much in common. Snitker is from Illinois, Anthopoulos from Montreal. Snitker is more than 22 years older than Anthopoulos, who isn't one of those GMs who watches batting practice daily. He mostly leaves the on-field stuff to Snitker and his players. Much had to happen for these men to be working for this club, but here they are and how lucky are we?

As a tandem, Schuerholz and Cox oversaw 14 consecutive first-place finishes. Only 10 to go for AA and Snit. ■

Both veterans of the franchise, Brian Snitker and Freddie Freeman celebrate the Braves' first World Series appearance since 1999. (Curtis Compton/The Atlanta Journal-Constitution)

NL PLAYOFFS

National League Division Series Game 1
October 8, 2021 • Milwaukee, Wisconsin
Brewers 2, Braves 1

THE BATTLE BEGINS

Braves Lose Pitching Duel to Brewers in Game 1 of NLDS

By Gabriel Burns

The expected Game 1 pitching duel between the Braves and Brewers lived up to the hype.

Charlie Morton and Corbin Burnes matched one another pitch-for-pitch, trading zeroes for six innings. Burnes exited with a stalemate as Morton continued onward – until two hitters into the seventh.

Avisail Garcia was hit by a pitch to open the frame. Four pitches later, Rowdy Tellez became a Brewers postseason hero with a monstrous two-run shot off a middle-placed fastball from Morton to snap a scoreless tie and end Morton's outing.

The Braves lost Game 1 of the National League Division Series 2-1. They haven't won a postseason series after losing the first game since 1999; they'll have to buck that trend to advance to their second consecutive NL Championship Series.

"We knew this ballgame was going to be rough," manager Brian Snitker said. "The runs would be at a premium. And they were. It was exactly what I thought was, going in, that this game would be, somebody got a big hit. And a lot of times most of the big hits in the postseason, they're homers. They hit one, and we didn't. But it was a good ballgame."

Tellez's smash spoiled one of the great outings in Morton's illustrious postseason career. A renowned big-game pitcher, Morton came out firing, striking out five of the first six Brewers. He allowed one hit – Lorenzo Cain's one-out single in the third – over his first four frames.

Morton threw 50 pitches in that time, recording eight of 12 outs via strikeout. He allowed three Brewers base

runners over six innings before his final sequence. He erased a leadoff walk in the sixth by retiring the top of the Brewers' lineup 1-2-3, which gave Snitker the confidence to keep Morton on the mound for the seventh.

"He was outstanding," Snitker said of Morton. "It was about as good as you can get. Threw one pitch that he probably would take back. But other than that, shoot, it was awesome."

On his decision to keep Morton in the game entering the seventh: "I talked to him. He said he felt good. If he'd have had 10 or 15 more pitches, I probably wouldn't have. But I thought he was in a zone, in an area where all year long we've let him go back. It was one pitch in the thing. I wouldn't second guess because you have to take your hat off to the hitter (Tellez). He didn't miss it, didn't foul it off."

Morton had both seventh-inning hitters with two strikes before the hit by pitch and homer.

"I hit Avi with the heater; I just yanked that four-seamer to Rowdy," Morton said. "I felt like I threw the ball well. I worked into the seventh inning, felt like we were in a really good spot. And then I hit Avi in a two-strike count, and I grooved one to Rowdy with a two-strike count."

The Braves couldn't muster Morton any run support because of Burnes. A missed opportunity in the first inning loomed over the Braves' defeat.

Burnes started his outing by walking Braves sluggers Jorge Soler and Freddie Freeman. Burnes' 16th pitch – the fourth ball to Freeman – bounced to the backstop and allowed Soler to advance to third.

Yet Burnes required only six more pitches to escape

Starting pitcher Charlie Morton held the Brewers scoreless until the seventh inning of Game 1. (Curtis Compton/The Atlanta Journal-Constitution)

unscathed. Second baseman Ozzie Albies swung at a low-and-inside cutter that was grounded to first. Brewers first baseman Tellez then fired home to nab Soler, who ran on contact, resulting in a double play. Freeman advanced to third on a wild pitch, but third baseman Austin Riley struck out.

"That's a tough one when you're at third base," Snitker, a former third-base coach, said of Soler running. "I don't put it on him. Probably 95 percent of the guys would go on that. Because you can't react quick enough and think quick enough on that play right there. If that ball is tapped out in front of the plate, then you can shut it down. It's hard to shut down that ball right there. He had to make a good throw too. He made a decent throw. The catcher made a nice play. It's bang, bang, and so I'm not – he's fine right there."

So the Braves, despite having two on with none out and twice having a base runner at third, couldn't take the immediate lead. The squandered scoring chance loomed over the game as Morton and Burnes traded zeroes.

Burnes was off his A-game, missing the strike zone often while laboring through the first two frames. While he didn't allow a hit, he issued three walks and had a wild pitch (possibly two, though one was called a passed ball). He needed 40 pitches to record six outs, but kept the Braves off the board.

The Braves' first hit was outfielder Eddie Rosario's bloop single to open the fifth. Catcher Travis d'Arnaud grounded into a double play, which meant shortstop Dansby Swanson's ensuing single merely allowed the Braves to clear Morton in the order.

Milwaukee lifted Burnes at 91 pitches for pinch-hitter Daniel Vogelbach, who led off the sixth. If the series goes to a decisive Game 5, the Braves should see the Brewers' ace again.

Joc Pederson, pinch-hitting for reliever Luke Jackson, smacked a solo shot off righty Adrian Houser in the eighth to trim the Braves' deficit to one. It was Pederson's 10th career postseason homer. Brewers closer Josh Hader allowed two base runners, walking Freeman and surrendering a single to Riley, but closed it by coaxing former teammate Orlando Arcia into a game-ending grounder.

"In the playoffs, runs are pretty hard to come by," Pederson said. "There are a lot of good pitchers. I think as a team we need to do better and take advantage of every opportunity we can because the pitchers are good." ∎

Joc Pederson hits a solo home run in the eighth inning, the only run the Braves would score in their 2-1 loss. (Curtis Compton/The Atlanta Journal-Constitution)

National League Division Series Game 2

October 9, 2021 • Milwaukee, Wisconsin

Braves 3, Brewers 0

GETTING EVEN

Fried Dominates as Braves Win, Even Series with Brewers

By Gabriel Burns

Max Fried, as he did throughout the Braves' dash to October, delivered in his team's time of need. And his dominance in Game 2 on October 9 flipped the National League Division Series to the Braves' favor.

Behind Fried and their best hitters sparking the offense, the Braves defeated the Brewers 3-0 in Game 2 of the best-of-five NLDS. It evened the series at 1-1 as it shifted to Truist Park for the next two games – giving the Braves the possibility of winning on their home field.

The first two games were dominated by strong pitching – as expected. Charlie Morton, Corbin Burnes, Fried and Brandon Woodruff, along with the teams' bullpens, have resulted in six runs scored across the first two contests.

"It's two really well-rounded, solid clubs going at it," manager Brian Snitker said. "Today we got some big hits. It was another really good ballgame."

Fried was exceptional. The southpaw, whose 1.74 second-half ERA was best in the majors, picked up where he left off in the regular season. He held the Brewers to three hits over six scoreless innings. He outdueled Brewers starter Brandon Woodruff, whose 2.56 ERA was fourth lowest in the NL.

The Brewers stayed within striking distance throughout the afternoon, but Fried's impeccable command made their two-run deficit feel insurmountable. Fried had a three-ball count three times, with none of those hitters reaching base. He struck out nine and didn't issue a walk.

Two of the three hits he surrendered were on soft contact.

"It's just a ton of strikes," Brewers manager Craig Counsell said of Fried. "There's no free pitches for hitters. He doesn't leave stuff in the middle. The slider is a really good pitch to the right-handed hitters, kind of bears on their hands, and he pairs that with a fastball on their hands. He's just a really good pitcher, executing a lot of pitches. It spells a tough night for the offense."

Snitker lifted Fried for pinch-hitter Joc Pederson with two out and none out in the seventh. After getting punished for keeping Morton into the seventh in Game 1, Snitker played it conservatively and removed Fried at 81 pitches with a three-run advantage.

"The biggest thing about that, he left it out there in the sixth," Snitker said. "He went through the meat of their lineup and expended what I felt was a lot of energy right there in a real big moment in playoff baseball. Charlie has been through this 100 times. Max is just cutting his teeth with all this."

The decision looked shaky for a moment, with the Brewers mounting a two-out rally against reliever Luke Jackson. Snitker turned to lefty Tyler Matzek with two on and two out, and the southpaw struck out Tyrone Taylor on four pitches (the one called ball was still in the strike zone) to end the threat.

Matzek saw the first two Brewers reach in the eighth. He again escaped, retiring the next three in order, capped with a strikeout of Avisail Garcia.

Starting pitcher Max Fried gets a fist bump from catcher Travis d'Arnaud after recording six scoreless innings against the Brewers. (Curtis Compton/The Atlanta Journal-Constitution)

"This guy's pitched so many big innings for us," Snitker said. "He's not a match-up guy either. He's got really good numbers against right-handed hitters. The slug against him is in the .200s, I think. He's pitched some really big innings for us over the last couple of years. So that was huge. And those were going through the teeth of their lineup in a very stressful situation."

Will Smith pitched around two base runners to finish the game, completing the Braves' bounce-back from a Game 1 defeat.

Morton, who started Game 1, and Fried have met lofty expectations. Both put the Braves in position to defeat the Brewers' co-aces Burnes and Woodruff. Morton and Fried were a primary reason the Braves felt they could go on an October run. They showed why in Wisconsin.

Morton and Fried combined to hold the Brewers to two runs on six hits over 12 innings. They struck out 18 and walked one.

The Braves obtained their first lead of the series in the third inning. Leadoff man Jorge Soler ignited the offense, ripping a 111-mph one-out double down the third-base line.

First baseman Freddie Freeman wouldn't let his team squander another chance with a runner in scoring position (they were 0-for-6 in such opportunities this series before the inning). He popped a two-strike curveball from Woodruff into right field. Soler, thrown out at home in the first inning of Game 1, was safe this time and gave the Braves a 1-0 lead.

Second baseman Ozzie Albies smashed a ball that bounced off the top of the right-field wall. Albies just missed a homer, but the double brought Freeman home for the team's second run. The All-Star later did push-ups, saying he needs to get stronger to get that ball over the fence.

"Tomorrow's an off day - I might work out from 8.00 a.m. until 8:00 p.m.," Albies said. "That ball has to go out."

The Braves had one run on four hits in Game 1. They had two runs on three hits in the third inning of Game 2.

While Soler and Freeman were held hitless in the Braves' 2-1 Game 1 loss, they drew a combined three walks. The duo had two hits, scored two runs and walked once in Game 2, setting the table for the crucial third inning.

Third baseman Austin Riley gave the Braves additional breathing room with a 424-foot homer off Woodruff in the sixth. It was Riley's second postseason home run following his blast in Game 1 of the 2020 NL Championship Series.

It wasn't an elimination game, but it was close to a must-win. The Braves split in Milwaukee, creating the possibility of ending the series with two victories at home. They prevented the Brewers from securing consecutive wins with Burnes and Woodruff starting. The Braves will see Burnes again if they return to Milwaukee for a decisive Game 5, but they'll try to prevent that scenario in the upcoming week.

"You come on the road in the playoffs, you want to split," Snitker said. "Obviously you'd love to take two, but if you split, that's a good thing." ∎

Max Fried limited the Brewers to three hits during his Game 2 outing, garnering praise from teammates and manager Brian Snitker. (Curtis Compton/The Atlanta Journal-Constitution)

National League Division Series Game 3
October 11, 2021 • Atlanta, Georgia
Braves 3, Brewers 0

CLUTCH IN PEARLS

Pederson's Pinch-Hit Blast Gives Braves the Win, 2-1 Series Lead

By Gabriel Burns

The Braves' July trades changed their season. And one just changed the National League Division Series.

In a series starved for offense, Joc Pederson has been an exception. "Joctober," as it's called, is alive and well in Atlanta. Pederson's three-run pinch-hit homer lifted the Braves past the Brewers 3-0 in Game 3 of the best-of-five series at Truist Park. The Braves are one win away from advancing to their second consecutive NL Championship Series.

Game 3 unfolded similarly to the past two contests. Starters Ian Anderson and Freddy Peralta were matching zeroes. The contest changed in the fifth when the Brewers, trying to spark an anemic offense, lifted Peralta at 57 pitches for a pinch-hitter with two in scoring position.

The decision backfired twice. Milwaukee didn't manage a run in that frame, wasting their best scoring chance against Anderson, then saw reliever Adrian Houser serve Pederson a middle-high fastball that was deposited into the right-field seats. A scoreless tie became a three-run Braves lead.

A stat to summarize the series: The teams are a combined 2-for-33 with runners in scoring position – but the Braves have both hits. The Brewers are 0-for-16 in that department. Their offensive struggles parallel the Reds' woes during their wild-card series against the Braves in 2020, when Cincinnati failed to score over two contests and the Braves' few key hits were enough.

Entering the series, attention centered on pitching – with an acknowledgement that the Braves' offense was vastly more potent than Milwaukee's. While the Brewers' pitching has mostly nerfed the Braves' bats, the offensive advantage has still come to light. Pederson is an advantage by himself, outproducing the Brewers, 4-2.

The longtime Dodger knows nothing but meaningful games. His first October with the Braves is off to a dashing start: Pederson is 3-for-3 with two homers. While the slugger was the least effective of Jorge Soler, Adam Duvall and Eddie Rosario – the July newcomer outfielders – in the regular season, he's been the difference when it matters most.

"He's been in these situations a lot, No. 1," manager Brian Snitker said. "No. 2, that guy's got no heartbeat at all. It's like he's on the playground. Playing against him in the postseason last few years, you could tell that. He just slows things down and has his at-bat. It's really focused. He's a very talented young man. He's been very successful in the postseason."

Pederson is an adored teammate. The team constantly remarks about his personality and energy. He showed it in late August, when he showed up to the Braves' series at Dodger Stadium with blonde hair. He's shown it in the past week while wearing pearls around his neck. Pederson has repeatedly been asked about the "why" behind his pearls, and while he charms in his answers, he rarely elaborates beyond saying he bought them from his jeweler.

"I don't know if I have a media answer for that," Pederson said when asked to describe his personality. "I'm just me."

In the past few days, Pederson's play has done the

Joc Pederson celebrates his three-run pinch-hit home run that decided Game 3. Pederson's style and prowess inspired countless Braves fans to wear pearls of their own in support. (Hyosub Shin/The Atlanta Journal-Constitution)

talking. Runs are at a premium in this series, and Pederson has been a godsend for the Braves.

Early indications suggested Game 3 could become another memorable Braves postseason disaster after a baserunning gaffe. The Braves opened the second with third baseman Austin Riley's soft infield single and outfielder Adam Duvall's hit, positioning them to get an early run off Peralta.

Outfielder Eddie Rosario advanced Riley to third. Catcher Travis d'Arnaud then slapped a flyout into left field, allowing Riley to run home. But Duvall was nabbed inexplicably running to second, resulting in an inning-ending double play that erased the run.

Ultimately, it proved inconsequential. The Braves seemingly had a small margin for error Monday, but Pederson's blast rendered Duvall's miscue a footnote. Such is possible with the Braves' mashing ability.

"That wasn't a good play by Adam," Snitker said. "I talked to him about it. He agrees. It was probably just getting caught up in the moment. That's one of the guys, he doesn't make mistakes. He did right there. If he came in here right now and sat down, he'd say, 'I screwed up.'"

The Brewers squandered a scoring chance two innings later. They had runners at second and third against Anderson in the fourth. Shortstop Dansby Swanson, a Gold Glove contender, made an eye-popping diving stop to prevent Lorenzo Cain's ball from reaching the outfield. Swanson fired home for out No. 1.

"When you have a defense behind you like we do, you know you're never out of an inning," Anderson said. "You know you've got a chance to get out of any jam. I think they showed that with the diving play he made."

Then the game-deciding sequence: Brewers manager Craig Counsell lifted Peralta for pinch-hitter Daniel Vogelbach. Peralta, who surrendered three hits in four innings, would've faced the bottom of the Braves' lineup before the third time through the order. Counsell knew his team couldn't afford another missed offensive opportunity. He was right.

Vogelbach hit a chopper to third and Luis Urias was caught in a rundown between third and home for the second out. Kolten Wong, who's among the many Brewers enduring a tough series, lined out to first to end the inning.

Anderson, meanwhile, pitched his best outing since returning from a shoulder injury in late August. He allowed three hits across five scoreless innings, striking out six without issuing a walk. In his second October, he appeared just as comfortable as a year ago, when he had a 0.96 ERA over four playoff starts.

The 23-year-old is the first pitcher with four scoreless starts of at least four innings in his first five postseason starts.

"Every situation he's handled beautifully, even throughout this year with some of the adversity and the ups and downs and the little shoulder injury that had him on IL for a little bit," Swanson said. "To come back and really find his groove, especially towards the end and into the playoffs, it's just remarkable to see a guy compete like that. That's what it comes down to, the compete factor. I love being able to play behind him. Love having him on our team. Just a joy to watch and to see the growth each and every day."

The Braves' starting pitching has been spectacular through three games. Charlie Morton, Max Fried and Ian Anderson have combined to allow two runs on nine hits over 17 innings. They've struck out 24 and walked one.

When the Braves clinched the NL East, they said they believed a postseason run was possible largely because of their starting pitching. Those starters – along with a bullpen that hasn't allowed a run in nine innings – have met or exceeded every hope, outdueling a staff that's arguably the best in MLB.

"I think it's unheard of to throw up that many zeros for our pitching staff in a playoff series," Pederson said. "(The Brewers have) definitely had opportunities to capitalize. And our pitchers are making quality pitches to get out of jams, which takes a lot of heart. You've got to tip your hat to that." ∎

Shortstop Dansby Swanson reacts after completing a double play to end the eighth inning against the Brewers. (Curtis Compton/The Atlanta Journal-Constitution)

National League Division Series Game 4
October 12, 2021 • Atlanta, Georgia
Braves 5, Brewers 4

'THE PERFECT ENDING'

The Great Freddie Freeman Leads His Team into the NLCS

By Mark Bradley

A careening Game 4 was set right at the end. With one majestic swing, the noblest Brave of all sent a Josh Hader slider flying deep into the night. It carried over the wall in center field, and it carried these Braves, the team that took forever to break .500, into the National League Championship Series for a second consecutive season. Freddie Freeman did what he has been doing for a decade, though never in a moment quite like this.

The Braves won the game 5-4 and this NL Division Series 3-1. They won seven fewer games than the Brewers over the regular season, but never in the series did Milwaukee seem the better side. The Braves got hot when they needed to get hot, and they believe they can beat anyone. They may well be right.

Braves manager Brian Snitker said: "It was just the perfect ending ... I'll never forget this."

Hader hadn't yielded a homer to a left-handed hitter this season. He has now. Said Freeman: "I really wasn't looking for a pitch. I was just looking for something up. He threw three sliders to Dansby (Swanson) and a couple to Eddie Rosario. I thought he might be going slider-happy. I was looking up and in, not down and away."

There was no doubt where this blast was headed. There was, however, some concern on Freeman's part as he rounded the bases. "I was trying not to fall over," he said.

Then: "This is what you dream of as a kid, hitting a home run to win in the playoffs."

Game 4 came as a relief: Something finally happened. Not to sound persnickety, but there hadn't been much to games 1-3. The team that scored first won. In Games 2 and 3, the team that scored won. The winning side in games 1 and 3 got all its runs on one swing. There was a lot of swinging and missing, some bad base running and a heapin' helpin' of pitchin' – which is standard fare for October, but it doesn't make for must-see TV.

Game 4 was different. Game 4 was wild. For the second day running, the Braves' Adam Duvall took off running and handed his team an inexplicable out. The umpires huddled to review an adjudged foul out – one of the few foul outs to feature an assist, the ball having bounded from catcher Omar Narvaez's mitt to third baseman Luis Urias' glove, or did it? – and then decided they couldn't overturn the non-catch because you're not allowed to review infield catches. Got that?

The talking point before the game involved Charlie Morton, who started Game 1 three days earlier in Milwaukee. Snitker opted to bring Morton back on short rest, which made some sense, given that Morton has been terrific in postseasons of late. At 3:41 p.m., an MLB press release sent those of us in the press box scurrying for our keyboards. The Braves' Jorge Soler had tested positive for COVID-19. This affected the batting order, Dansby Swanson being redeployed as a leadoff man, and the outfield, Guillermo Heredia getting a start.

Back to Morton. He wasn't as sharp as in Game 1 – that can happen with short rest – and exited after 3⅓ innings, at which point Game 4 went nuts.

The Brewers fashioned an actual rally against Morton and then Jesse Chavez, giving them a 2-0 lead. The Braves

Freddie Freeman's solo home run off Josh Hader capped off a wild Game 4 against the Brewers.
(Curtis Compton/The Atlanta Journal-Constitution)

tied the score forthwith, chasing Milwaukee starter Eric Lauer and giving this series its first tie that wasn't 0-0. Milwaukee responded with another massive two-run homer by Rowdy Tellez – say this for Tellez: When he hits one, it stays hit – off a Huascar Ynoa slider that fit the industry description of a "cement mixer," in that it spins slowly until it gets whacked.

Back came the Braves. There was nothing majestic about their second two-run inning. They loaded the bases on an infield single, a walk and a hit batsman. They cut the lead to 4-3 on Joc Pederson's groundout. (The pinch-hitting, pearl-wearing star of the series had finally gotten a start.) They tied it on Travis d'Arnaud's smash that ducked under Tellez's first-baseman's mitt.

At this point, play was suspended so everyone could take a nap. OK, I made that up. But the series that saw nine runs scored in Games 1-3 had just offered eight in two innings. Everybody was a bit winded, and the pace of play showed it. The first four innings took more than 2½ hours. Game 1 in its entirety required three hours on the nose.

At least the series had gotten interesting. The Brewers were fighting to play a Game 5 in Milwaukee. The Braves were laboring to get this over with. When Freddie Freeman and Ozzie Abiles singled in the sixth, Milwaukee manager Craig Counsell turned to his bullpen for the third time on the night, but the pitcher who appeared was Brandon Woodruff, starter and loser of Game 2.

This marked Woodruff's first relief stint since 2018, and the batter he faced was familiar – Austin Riley, who hit a home run off him in Game 2. (So: two days' rest!) Woodruff threw one pitch. Riley topped it to third. Inning over. Still 4-all.

The game had begun at 5:16 in sunshine. By now it was long past dark. Come the eighth, Counsell turned to Hader, who's usually only a ninth-inning man. Hader struck out Rosario and Swanson. Up stepped Freeman, big lefty hitter against big lefty pitcher. Hader opened with a slider. Freeman was dead on it, sending it flying over fence in center.

Most every swing this man takes is a thing of beauty. This was a work of art. Said Counsell: "It was their best against our best ... It's how our game is. It's how our game should be."

Said Snitker: "You couldn't script this. Freddie Freeman hit a home run off the best closer in the game." ∎

NLCS-bound for the second year running, the Braves take a celebratory photo at Truist Park following their 5-4 win over the Brewers. (Curtis Compton/The Atlanta Journal-Constitution)

National League Championship Series Game 1
October 16, 2021 • Atlanta, Georgia
Braves 3, Dodgers 2

DOUBLE VISION

Austin Riley's Walk-Off Hit Gives Braves 1-0 Over Dodgers in NLCS

By Gabriel Burns

For the second consecutive year, the Braves defeated the Dodgers in Game 1 of the National League Championship Series. This time, they'll hope the ultimate result is different.

Hosting Game 1 at Truist Park, the Braves defeated the Dodgers 3-2 on third baseman Austin Riley's walk-off double off Blake Treinen that scored second baseman Ozzie Albies. It was Riley's first walk-off hit in his career.

"You dream of that as a little kid," Riley said. "It was huge. That was my first one ever. I've come up in quite a few situations earlier in the season and wasn't able to get it done, but to get it done tonight was awesome."

Albies made it possible by reaching on a soft hit and then swiping second base. Riley punished a middle-placed slider from Treinen down the left-field line to end it. It was also the second consecutive year Riley provided the go-ahead hit in Game 1 of the NLCS; his homer off Treinen in the ninth inning last year sparked the offense in a 5-1 victory.

"He's the big boss," Albies said of Riley. "Once I got on, I (said) I'm going (to steal) so I can be in scoring position for Riley. He's been hot. He's going to do the job. No doubt."

Braves starter Max Fried allowed two runs over six innings. The Dodgers' first four hits came on off-speed pitches from Fried. The lefty, who had MLB's best ERA in the second half of the regular season, uncharacteristically had to work through traffic. Six of the eight hits he allowed came with two strikes.

Yet Fried kept his team in it. He didn't log a clean frame but held the Dodgers to 1-for-6 with runners in scoring position. Despite lacking his A-grade stuff, Fried still didn't issue a walk for the third consecutive start.

"I felt like I was fighting myself at times, not executing two-strike pitches as well as I would have wanted, but I was working really well with (catcher) Travis (d'Arnaud) back there, really relied on him a lot, especially calling pitches later in that outing," Fried said. "I felt like he had a really good feel on that game and I really relied on him. Defense just made some really nice plays again. ... The only thing I was trying to do was just to keep it right there and give us an opportunity."

Fried pitched to contact – an emphasis during his emergence into a frontline starter – and let his defense help him. His outing finished with Albies making a leaping catch that prevented a ball from reaching the outfield and scoring the go-ahead run.

"I don't know that Max really felt like he was on tonight, but he just kept pitching, never gave in," manager Brian Snitker said. "And you get six innings; six innings is tough in a playoff game because it's just such an emotional and adrenaline-type driven outing. I thought he did great. He was really good and he had to really work through the sixth. That inning there wasn't an easy inning for him and he pretty much laid it out there to get through that inning."

The Braves struck quickly against the Dodgers, who deployed a bullpen game. Outfielder Eddie Rosario,

Austin Riley's walk-off double off of Dodgers reliever Blake Treinen scored Ozzie Albies to win Game 1. It was the first walk-off hit of Riley's career. (Hyosub Shin/The Atlanta Journal-Constitution)

moved to leadoff with Jorge Soler's absence, opened with a single against Corey Knebel. He stole second as first baseman Freddie Freeman struck out.

Rosario moved to third on Albies' grounder to the right side of the infield. He scored on Knebel's wild pitch that eluded catcher Will Smith and bounced to the backstop. Snitker's decision to move Rosario to leadoff paid immediate dividends.

But unlike the Brewers, who struggled mightily to produce offense against the Braves in their Division Series, the Dodgers could swiftly respond. They did so with a pair of two-out hits – an AJ Pollock double and Chris Taylor single – off Fried to even the score.

Smith homered off an 0-2 fastball from Fried in the fourth to put the Dodgers ahead. Riley answered in the bottom of the frame with a rocketed solo shot off Tony Gonsolin to reset the score.

Despite a leadoff bloop double from Taylor, Tyler Matzek again showed why he's one of the best lefty relievers in MLB. Pinch-hitter Austin Barnes laid down a perfect bunt to give the Dodgers a runner at third with one out. Matzek responded by getting former MVP Mookie Betts to pop out in foul ground. He then struck out Trea Turner with a low slider.

"I've got a hundred percent confidence in Tyler," Fried said. "He's been doing it all year. When you have a lefty that comes in and is in the high 90s and has a wipeout slider, you're pretty confident that if you just hold the game tied, or with a little lead, that he's going to keep holding it."

"He's thrown every game this whole playoffs and obviously he's been extremely important to our success, so anytime that I can hand the ball off to him it's probably a good thing."

Luke Jackson followed with a perfect eighth. Jackson's regular season success has carried into October. He's pitched in all five of the Braves' games this postseason, allowing three hits and no runs.

Will Smith followed with his fourth scoreless inning in the postseason, helped by Taylor's base-running error in which he was caught between second and third following Cody Bellinger's pinch-hit single. The mistake loomed large for the Dodgers, who also went 1-for-8 with runners in scoring position.

"I think by the book he should have probably stayed," Dodgers manager Dave Roberts said. "It was hit softly. It was kind of towards the gap, and so I felt that he thought he had a good read on it."

"It's one of those where you got to pick. You either are going to go hard, and I don't know if Joc (Pederson) would have thrown to third right there and just conceded that base, or just hold up and two outs and give Mookie a chance (Betts was on deck). But I think right there he was kind of caught in between. That's kind of when you get in trouble." ∎

Left fielder Eddie Rosario catches a fly ball off the bat of the Dodgers' Will Smith in the sixth inning of Game 1. (Hyosub Shin/The Atlanta Journal-Constitution)

National League Championship Series Game 2
October 17, 2021 • Atlanta, Georgia
Braves 5, Dodgers 4

ANOTHER NEW HERO
Again the Braves Lead L.A. 2-0, and This Time It Feels Different
By Mark Bradley

Just like last year, the Braves lead the Dodgers 2-0 in the National League Championship Series. But there's a chance – a very good chance – this year is not like last year. These Braves look much less likely to waste a lead. As for the regal Dodgers … well, they just blew a lead. They aren't the team they were a year ago.

Eddie Rosario, of whom few Atlantans had heard before the Braves added him at the trade deadline, had four hits in Game 2, the last coming off Dodgers closer Kenley Jansen and going unfielded by shortstop Corey Seager. It was scored a game-winning single, but on another night Seager makes that play. He didn't this time. For the second consecutive night, the Braves won on a ninth-inning walk-off hit.

Said Rosario: "When I saw Seager in the middle, I went 'oh.' But he missed the ball."

Without Ronald Acuna and Marcell Ozuna, the Braves aren't the team they were a year ago, either. Somehow they're better. They believe they're as good as the Dodgers. They might well be right. They trailed 4-2 in the bottom of the eighth. They won 5-4. They held the Dodgers to four hits on a night when the Braves' starter lasted three innings.

Freddie Freeman doesn't have a hit in the series, having struck out seven times. His team leads 2-0. Said Joc Pederson, the improbable catalyst: "When we're all pulling on the same string, things happen. No person feels like it's on his shoulders to have to get the job done. It's a different guy every night."

Max Scherzer is among the best pitchers of this century, but the Braves have seen him a lot – he spent 6⅔ seasons with Washington of the National League East – and his ERA over 27 games against Atlanta was 3.88. That's not anywhere near awful, but it's not Scherzer-like. His career ERA: 3.16. The Braves knew Sunday wouldn't be an easy night. They also knew they weren't apt to see anything they hadn't seen a dozen times already.

Ian Anderson didn't have it in Game 2. It happens to everybody. It's the first time it has happened to him over two postseasons. (Remember, he started Game 7 against the Dodgers last October.) He fought his changeup, his money pitch. He did well to get through three innings. L.A. generated six baserunners, three on walks.

Mookie Betts led off with a blooper Dansby Swanson couldn't snare. Corey Seager slugged the next pitch, a curve, over the fence in right-center. The thought occurred that the Dodgers were miffed at losing Game 1, but here again we cite pesky facts: These teams have played nine postseason games over 13 months; the Braves have won five. They aren't Vanderbilt – though Swanson is an alum – to L.A.'s Alabama.

We also wonder if, like the contemporary Alabama, these Dodgers aren't a lesser version of themselves. They're missing Clayton Kershaw, Trevor Bauer and Max Muncy. Justin Turner didn't start Game 2, having developed a stiff neck. After opening Game 2 with a single and a home run, the Dodgers managed two hits over the next eight innings, one against the Braves' seven relievers. By the bottom of the fifth, L.A.'s lead was gone. So was Scherzer.

Austin Riley drew a walk, Scherzer's one and only, in the fourth. Up stepped the man who has touched off a run on second-hand stores, everyone scrounging for a strand

Joc Pederson's two-run home run off of Max Scherzer in the fourth inning traveled 451 feet. Pederson's blast tied Game 2, 2-2. (Hyosub Shin/The Atlanta Journal-Constitution)

of pearls, or facsimiles thereof, to wear to the ballpark. The man himself believes we in the media have made too much of his fashion sense. Having worked previously near Hollywood, Pederson knows full well there's no such thing as a story we can't overblow.

The drive Pederson launched off Scherzer cannot be understated. The wearer of pearls turned on a curveball that hung just enough for him to drive it 451 miles. (OK, 451 feet. Still, this was crushed.) "Got the boys back in it," Pederson said, and that's the thing: These Braves are never not in it.

Said manager Brian Snitker: "If you leave early, you'll hear it on your car radio and miss the best part of the game. These guys play a tough 27 (outs)."

In the fifth, Scherzer threw two fastballs to Swanson, the second of which was scorched up the middle for a single. Those four-seamers were clocked at under 93 mph. When the night began, Scherzer was topping 94 mph. Manager Dave Roberts lifted the famous pitcher in the fifth, Scherzer having needed 79 pitches to record 10 outs.

Snitker pulled Anderson after three innings. TBS cameras caught the manager speaking at length to his pitcher, Snitker having seen what everyone else saw. Anderson's grit kept a game that started poorly from going way wrong, but Anderson's grit wouldn't be enough for the Braves to win. They needed another banner effort from their bullpen. They got it.

Said Snitker: "We planned for everything but a short start, and it still worked out."

Tyler Matzek entered with two out in the sixth and Chris Taylor on third base. Jacob Webb had opened the inning by walking Taylor, but he induced Cody Bellinger to fly out and AJ Pollock to whiff. Matzek struck out Albert Pujols to hold the tie, making one of the sport's all-time greats look feeble.

The seventh began with Betts walking and stealing second. Matzek fanned Seager and Trea Turner. Snitker summoned Luke Jackson to face Justin Turner, pressed into pinch-hitting duty. Jackson plunked J. Turner with a slider, loading the bases. Taylor drove a four-seamer clocked at

96.9 mph into center field. Guillermo Heredia, who'd just entered as half of a double switch, couldn't glove it.

Two runs scored. For a moment, it appeared more would, the ball having skipped past Heredia. That the ball died, forcing J. Turner to hold at third, proved monumental. The Braves tied it in the eighth off Julio Urías, who last year closed Game 7 of the NLCS and who won 20 games as a starter this season. Rosario singled against the shift, moving to second on Freeman's fly ball. Rosario scored on Ozzie Albies' single, also against the shift.

"I did a really good job on the slide," Rosario said, and he did. But Steven Souza, inserted into right field after striking out as a pinch-hitter, made a lousy throw. Sense a theme? The Braves are making plays. The Dodgers aren't.

Albies scored on Riley's double to left-center. Tied again. Trea Turner led off the ninth by hitting a fly ball off Will Smith that Rosario caught at the wall. Smith struck out the next two Dodgers, his namesake included. Last October, the NLCS turned on the Game 5 homer by L.A.'s Will Smith off Atlanta's. This time the bearded Will had his way.

Bottom of the ninth. Travis d'Arnaud broke his bat but singled up the middle off Brusdar Graterol. Swanson put down a poor bunt that led to pinch-runner Cristian Pache being thrown out at second. Heredia grounded to third, pushing Swanson to second with two out. Jansen entered and threw one pitch. Rosario smacked it at, and past, Seager.

Six nights earlier, the chants at Truist Park were "Freddie!" This time Braves fans dropped the "Fr." They had yet another new hero. This team is headed west knowing it can't lose the series in L.A. I'm thinking this team won't lose it anywhere. ■

Ozzie Albies sprints home to score the tying run on Austin Riley's double to left-center in the eighth inning of Game 2. (Curtis Compton/The Atlanta Journal-Constitution)

National League Championship Series Game 3
October 19, 2021 • Los Angeles, California
Dodgers 6, Braves 5

EIGHTH INNING AGONY
Braves Lose Game 3 in their L.A. House of Horrors

By Michael Cunningham

Dodger Stadium is one of those ballparks that sits in the middle of a vast parking lot. It's an old, huge, no-frills venue that stands out during this era of smaller and newer stadiums with nicer amenities.

When I come here I can't help but think about the ugly part of the stadium's history: hundreds of families, most of them Mexican-American, violently displaced and Brooklyn Dodgers owner Walter O'Malley eventually getting land earmarked for public purpose for cheap. I shouldn't like Dodger Stadium for those reasons, but honestly, I've always loved this place.

The Braves apparently do not like Dodger Stadium, even though they should. It's a place that favors pitching, which long has been the foundation for the Braves. Yet for so long the Braves have come here and lost to the Dodgers, whether they got good pitching or not.

They were so close to changing that in Game 3. The Braves were five outs away from taking a 3-0 lead in the best-of-seven National League Championship Series. Historically, that's a near-insurmountable lead.

Then Cody Bellinger belted a three-run homer off Luke Jackson to tie the score in the eighth inning, and Mookie Betts hit a two-out, RBI double to send the Dodgers to a 6-5 victory.

The Braves still lead the series 2-1, but the rejuvenated Dodgers can draw on good history. They came back to beat the Braves in last year's NLCS after trailing 2-0 and 3-1. They've now won eight consecutive games and 11 of 12 (including playoffs) against the Braves at Dodger Stadium.

And they get two more chances to do it again before the series returns to Atlanta.

Last year's NLCS was played on a neutral field in Texas. The return to stadiums with partisan supporters helped the Braves win Games 1 and 2 at Truist Park. The Dodgers got a similar boost while taking a 2-0 lead in the first inning of Game 3. The Braves quieted their fans by taking leads of 4-2 in the fourth and 5-2 in the fifth.

"We were dead in the water," Dodgers manager Dave Roberts said.

They suddenly came alive against Jackson in the eighth. Will Smith led off with a single and AJ Pollock got a hit with one out. Bellinger scored them by belting Jackson's 1-2 pitch out to right-center field. Chris Taylor followed with a single before Jesse Chavez replaced Jackson. Chavez gave up the RBI double to Betts.

What a crushing loss for the Braves. Starting pitcher Charlie Morton had added another effective postseason outing to a resume full of them. In Games 1 and 2, the Braves got little production from All-Star Freddie Freeman or the bottom half of the order. In Game 4, Freeman had three hits and a walk while No. 6 hitter Adam Duvall and No. 8 Dansby Swanson provided pop.

None of that ended up mattering because Jackson couldn't hold the lead. His fastball to Bellinger was above the strike zone.

"It hurts," Jackson said. "We lost the game because I made a couple bad pitches that some days are outs, and some days they're home runs. (But) to feel like this is like a dagger, no, this is just a speed bump in the road."

Adam Duvall strikes out to end Game 3. The Braves led 5-2 going into the bottom of the eighth inning before the Dodgers scored four runs to take a 6-5 lead that proved to be the final score. (Curtis Compton/The Atlanta Journal-Constitution)

It could turn out that way for the Braves. Or it could be that they've once again let the Dodgers off the mat after they'd knocked them down.

The Dodgers took a 2-0 lead on Corey Seager's two-run homer in the first inning. They stranded runners on base in every subsequent inning except the seventh. Bellinger finally cashed in with his homer.

Dodgers fans who were dormant seeing all those scoring chances squandered erupted as their team once again bested the Braves in this stadium.

"That's as loud as I've heard Dodger Stadium," Roberts said.

The Braves didn't have to win this game. They don't need to win any of the three games here to advance to the World Series for the first time since 1999. But winning Game 3 would have drastically improved their outlook even beyond the historical probabilities: 38 of 39 MLB teams that have led a series 3-0 lead went on to win.

Braves manager Brian Snitker is planning a so-called bullpen game for Game 4. That would have been a less-worrisome proposition with a 3-0 lead. The Braves have tough lefty Max Fried lined up for Game 5. Now they'll have to win Game 4 to have a chance to clinch with him starting.

The Braves took control of Game 3 after it started off looking like another letdown for them in Los Angeles. Their first two batters, Eddie Rosario and Freeman, reached on singles and Ozzie Albies smacked a line drive that was tailing away from Gavin Lux. But the center fielder snagged the ball and doubled up Rosario, who inexplicably was about two-thirds of the way to third base.

That was a potential run the Braves could have used later. Austin Riley struck out to end the Braves' first inning, so they didn't score after putting their first two runners on base. That sequence energized Dodgers fans. They were further invigorated by a stirring performance by a mariachi band paying homage to Dodgers reliever Joe Kelly.

The party kept going in the bottom of the inning. Morton walked Betts, the first batter, before Seager launched a hanging curveball an estimated 444 feet to center field. The Braves were down 2-0 to the Dodgers, same as in Game 2. It could have been worse: Morton

issued three consecutive walks with two outs to load the bases before Taylor lined out softly.

The Braves came back in the fourth inning, same as in Game 2. Freeman led off with a single and, with one out, Riley smacked right-hander Walker Buehler's fastball high and deep to right-center field. Lux got twisted up tracking the ball — maybe he lost it in the sun — and dropped it near the wall.

The play was ruled a double for Riley. Instead of a runner at first with two outs, the Braves had runners at second and third with one out. That was the beginning of Buehler's unraveling.

Pederson hit a hard single to score Freeman — home plate umpire Jerry Meals called a ball on what looked like strike three — and Duvall's broken-bat hit brought home Riley. Buehler walked Travis d'Arnaud on four pitches before Swanson hit a sizzling ground ball that glanced off shortstop Seager's glove for an RBI single.

Buehler walked Rosario to score another run. Roberts pulled Buehler for Alex Vesia, who got Freeman to fly out to end the Braves' fourth. The Braves added another run in the fifth. Albies led off with a single against Corey Knebel and the next batter, Riley, walked. Phil Bickford replaced Knebel and surrendered an RBI single to Duvall.

Those runs weren't enough for the Braves to finally win a big game at Dodger Stadium. If there can be a silver lining in the loss, it's that the Dodgers used nine pitchers. They are set to start Julio Urias in Game 4 after he blew a save chance as a reliever in Game 2.

The Braves still lead the series and they still can take it home with them. They have two more chances to win here, but first they'll have to get over blowing this one.

"They will be fine," Snitker said of his players. They will come out (and) they will be ready to play. They're going to prepare as always. We have lost tough games before and bounced back and done really good things."

They just haven't done it for a long time in Dodger Stadium, their L.A. house of horrors. ■

Braves reliever Luke Jackson gathers his thoughts on the mound during the eighth inning. Jackson recorded one out before yielding a three-run home run to Cody Bellinger that tied Game 3, 5-5. (Curtis Compton/The Atlanta Journal-Constitution)

National League Championship Series Game 4
October 20, 2021 • Los Angeles, California
Braves 9, Dodgers 2

EDDIE, SET, GO!
Braves Bounce Back, Pound Dodgers 9-2 in Game 4

By Gabriel Burns

The Braves have shown their resilience time and again throughout the 2021 season. They provided another reminder of their mental fortitude in Game 4 of the NLCS, and they're one win from a World Series berth as a result.

After a devastating defeat in Game 3, the Braves bounced back with a 9-2 victory over the Dodgers to take a 3-1 lead in the best-of-seven series. This series has unfolded in the same fashion as the 2020 NLCS: The Braves won the first two, suffered a brutal loss in Game 3 but rebounded to win Game 4.

The Braves will try to end the similarities there and prevent a repeat of last year, when the Dodgers won three consecutive games to advance.

"We're a different team," manager Brian Snitker said. "We were really good last year. I think the difference is our starting pitching is more solidified this year. Our bullpen guys, all they do is answer the phone and get ready. And I ride them. I told them all they got saddle cinches on their sides because I have tightened that thing so hard riding them. They have done a great job.

"So the core group and the makeup of all this club is right on par from what we've had. It's cool. I think the core group of our guys make it easy for guys to come in and be a part of this. It's a great group of guys. I respect each and every one of them so much."

As Snitker alluded with his relievers comment, the Braves pitched a bullpen game to perfection in Game 4. Their offense did more than enough to supplement their arms, led by the Braves' own version of Mr. October in outfielder Eddie Rosario.

Rosario was the least heralded of the Braves' trade-deadline acquisitions. He was sidelined by an abdominal injury, and the team acquired him for a declining Pablo Sandoval. Now, with the NL pennant on the line, Rosario has been the Braves' best player.

He went 4-for-5, falling a double shy of his second cycle this season. In the NLCS, Rosario is 10-for-17 with a triple, two homers, two walks, six RBIs and five runs scored.

In a series featuring two teams who've met in back-to-back league championship series, including the defending champs with MLB's highest payroll, Rosario has been far and away the biggest standout.

"I'm still dreaming for bigger things," Rosario said. "I want more at this point and just dreaming for the next thing and hopefully we can get there."

Rosario became the first player in postseason history with two homers, a triple and a single in one game. For context about how rare that performance is, only one player has achieved those totals in two games: Hall of Famer Joe DiMaggio.

The Braves' bullpen game was a resounding success. Jesse Chavez, who opened the game after Huascar Ynoa was removed from the roster because of shoulder inflammation, pitched a perfect first. Lefty Drew Smyly followed by retiring the first seven Dodgers en route to three scoreless frames to begin his showing.

It was the best moment of the season for Smyly, the team's $11 million free-agent signing who was jettisoned from the rotation in September following his struggles.

Eddie Rosario celebrates his walk-off hit that scored Dansby Swanson in the ninth inning. Rosario was 4-for-5 on the night, a double shy of the cycle. (Curtis Compton/The Atlanta Journal-Constitution)

Smyly's last start, coincidently, was at Dodger Stadium when he surrendered four homers.

"I admire him so much and the professionalism and how he stays ready," Snitker said. "He's always ready to go. He's been through a lot. He's been a big part. I mean, he's won a lot of games for us, we won a lot of games that he started, and then we shied away from him and he just keeps working. It's like he'll do anything. He's a true professional to handle the situation like he has and to perform like he has. I got a lot of admiration for that man."

Smyly's outing ended one out into the fifth after he allowed consecutive singles from Justin Turner and Cody Bellinger. Veteran Chris Martin retired Chris Taylor before giving up a two-RBI single to pinch-hitter AJ Pollock, trimming the Braves' advantage to 5-2.

Lefty A.J. Minter pitched a perfect sixth against the heart of the Dodgers' lineup. He stayed for the seventh, surrendering a single to Albert Pujols. But Minter coaxed Turner into a double play – Turner suffered a leg injury running to first and left the game – then got Bellinger to fly out to center to end the inning.

"The biggest part, too, was Minter," Snitker said. "The two innings he got for us was huge."

Tyler Matzek and Will Smith pitched the final two innings, respectively, to close it for the Braves. The bullpen game resulted in just a four-hit showing for the Dodgers. The top four hitters in the Dodgers lineup were a combined 0-for-15.

The Braves took their lead in the second inning when Rosario, who was moved down to fifth in the lineup, hammered an 0-2 pitch from Julio Urias over the left-field wall. Center fielder Adam Duvall followed with his own blast, quickly making the score 2-0.

It was the first time the Braves have hit back-to-back home runs in the postseason since Oct. 3, 2002, in Game 2 of the NL Division Series against the Giants, when Javy Lopez and Vinny Castilla launched consecutive homers also in the second inning.

In the bottom of the frame, Duvall made a leaping grab at the center-field wall to rob Gavin Lux of an extra-base hit. It was that kind of night for the Braves, who disappointed the 53,025 on hand.

First baseman Freddie Freeman's 0-for-8 start to the series is long forgotten. After collecting three hits in Game 3, he blasted a towering solo homer off Urias in the third inning. Rosario's two-out triple allowed outfielder Joc Pederson to single home the Braves' fourth run.

Pederson's hit dropped in front of Lux in center. A natural infielder, Lux played the ball on a hop in front of him, frustrating Urias, who seemed to think Lux could've made the catch. It was Pederson's fourth RBI in the series and the third consecutive game in which he's produced a run. He has a hit in every game against his former club.

The Braves added their fifth run in the fifth after Rosario – who else? – singled and later scored on Duvall's sacrifice fly to Lux, who delivered a weak throw to the cutoff man. Freeman produced their sixth with an RBI double in the eighth. Rosario, who needed a double for the cycle, instead capped the night with a three-run blast off Tony Gonsolin.

"Three RBI is better than hitting a double," Rosario said.

Only 14 of the 89 teams to fall into a 3-1 hole in a best-of-seven series have rallied to advance. Just four times has that team overcome holes of 2-0 and 3-1 in the same series. Unfortunately for the Braves, the 2020 Dodgers achieved the feat, overcoming a 3-1 deficit in last year's NLCS.

"This is a whole different team, a whole different thing," Freeman said. "So if anybody's thinking about 2020, I think everybody wants to be in a 3-1 lead, so we'll take it and hopefully we – we got Max (Fried) going (in Game 5) so we're feeling pretty good."

These Braves can avenge that group with one more win – and they have Fried, Ian Anderson and Charlie Morton lined up if the series goes the distance. The Braves will try to prevent that, of course. They've largely dominated the series, outhitting, outpitching and outmanaging MLB's premier franchise over recent years.

"They just outplayed us in all facets," Dodgers manager Dave Roberts said. "Fried isn't going to feel sorry for us. He's going to go for the jugular. He's got great stuff and we got to compete. And to the question earlier, our backs are against the wall and no one's going to feel sorry. We got to find a way to stress him, get guys on base, and push them across, that's just the bottom line."

Fried, a Santa Monica native who grew up consuming baseball at Dodger Stadium, will try to live out his childhood dreams and help his team secure a World Series spot at Chavez Ravine.

"The last three years, Max has pretty much come into an ace starter," Freeman said. "So what he's done in the second half and pretty much over the whole course of the season after the first couple weeks every time you see No. 54 on that mound you got a real good feeling." ∎

Adam Duvall celebrates in the Braves' dugout after hitting a solo home run in the second inning of Game 4. (Curtis Compton/The Atlanta Journal-Constitution)

National League Championship Series Game 5
October 21, 2021 • Los Angeles, California
Dodgers 11, Braves 2

HOMEWARD BOUND

Dodgers Strike Back with a Big Win in Game 5, Returning Series to Atlanta

By Michael Cunningham

The Braves will say they're still in control of the National League Championship Series. That's true. Sure, that was a tough loss to the Dodgers in Game 5. But didn't the Braves blow Game 3 before coming back the next day and dominating the Dodgers?

That's the right outlook for the Braves as they head home after losing 11-2 at Dodger Stadium. They'll get up to two chances to beat the Dodgers at Truist Park and advance to the World Series.

"I think we're going to be fine," Braves slugger Freddie Freeman said.

Still, there's no downplaying it: The Braves squandered two good chances to leave L.A. with the pennant. They came here with a 2-0 series lead. They led Game 3 by three runs in the eighth inning before losing. The Braves had a chance to close the series in Game 5 with their best pitcher, Max Fried, and couldn't do it.

The two losses conjured the specter of the last year's NLCS. In that series, the Dodgers overcame deficits of 2-0 and 3-1 to beat the Braves. The Braves say that experience is one reason they're a different team. I believe them, but the only way the Braves can prove it is to finish off the Dodgers.

Win one game this weekend, and the Braves will advance to the World Series for the first time since 1999. Lose both, and the 2021 Braves will be added to the pile of postseason collapses for Atlanta sports teams.

About that history, Freeman said: "It's going to be the narrative, it seems, because every day it's brought up the last couple days. So I don't think we have a choice until we kill that narrative. We're up 3-2 and we're going home. That's a great position to be in."

The Braves overachieved to get this far. Coming from ahead to lose to the Dodgers again would take the luster off their run. There were good reasons to believe the Braves would win Game 5.

Nearly all their hitters came alive at the same time in Game 4. Dodgers manager Dave Roberts had used so many of his pitchers that he was forced to deploy a so-called bullpen game in Game 5. The Braves started Fried, MLB's ERA leader after the All-Star break.

Fried held the Dodgers to two runs over six innings in Game 1. He pitched six scoreless innings against Milwaukee in the previous round. Fried was back home in Southern California. There was every reason to expect him to be sharp.

Instead, Fried surrendered five earned runs over 4⅔ innings. He was staked to a 2-0 lead on Freddie Freeman's homer in the first inning. Fried gave up three runs on two home runs in the second, and allowed another run in the third. He just didn't have it.

"Physically, felt great," Fried said. "Just a really good, aggressive lineup (that) hit some pitches over the middle."

It's been a while since Fried struggled. It happened at the worst possible time. Chris Martin replaced Fried in the fifth inning and immediately gave up a two-run homer to Chris Taylor. The Dodgers piled on with five more runs after the Braves had conceded.

The Dodgers appeared to be a tired and beaten down team after the 9-2 loss in Game 4. The defending World Series champions got back up. By the end of the long night, the Braves seemed to be sapped of energy. The return home should rejuvenate them.

The Braves couldn't build on their fast start against right-handed pitcher Joe Kelly. They struck first, same as Game 4. Ozzie Albies singled with one out and Freeman followed with the homer. Worse for the Dodgers: Kelly left the game with forearm tightness after recording the second out and getting a 2-2 count against Adam Duvall.

Roberts summoned right-hander Evan Phillips. He struck out Duvall with one pitch. But the Dodgers trailed

Eddie Rosario is tagged out by Dodgers shortstop Corey Seager on a stolen base attempt in the third inning of Game 5. (Curtis Compton/The Atlanta Journal-Constitution)

2-0 and already were deep into their bullpen. The Braves had their ace on the mound.

Fried gave up a one-out single to the second batter he faced, Trea Turner, but got out of the inning with no issue. Fried's troubles began in the second. After Pollock's leadoff homer, Albert Pujols singled and Taylor hit another homer for a 3-2 Dodgers lead.

Cody Bellinger followed with a single. Fried struck out pinch hitter Steven Souza. That brought up Mookie Betts, L.A.'s most dangerous hitter. Betts drilled a fly ball to left field that Eddie Rosario tracked down and caught.

The Braves had a chance to erase their one-run deficit in the third inning. Rosario singled off lefty Alex Vesia, and Freeman was up with two outs, but Rosario got caught stealing to end the inning. Taylor's one-out, RBI single in the third inning pushed L.A.'s lead to 4-2.

Fried pitched a perfect fourth inning. By then the Dodgers had turned the lead over to Brusdar Graterol. Graterol only occasionally goes longer than an inning, but he did it with no problem against the Braves. He needed only six pitches to retire the Braves in order in the fourth inning.

Graterol's 1-2-3 fifth inning was over in eight pitches.

Getting those innings from Graterol was a big boost for the Dodgers. Taylor's two-run homer off Martin in the fifth gave them more breathing room. The Dodgers added six more runs. The Braves had no response. They managed to put only three runners on base after the first inning.

After the final out, Dodgers fans gave their team an ovation. They hope to see the Dodgers back here next week for another World Series. The Braves can make sure that doesn't happen. They still are in control of this series.

Braves right-hander Ian Anderson is scheduled to start Game 6. Charlie Morton is slated for Game 7, if necessary. Both pitchers will have extra rest.

Said Anderson: "We're still in a good spot. The vibes are still good, and we're going to hop on a flight, head home and be ready to play."

This time the Braves will get a chance to finish off the Dodgers in their packed ballpark instead of a neutral stadium in Texas. They say they're a different team than the one that faded against the Dodgers last October. The Braves get a chance to prove it come the weekend. ■

National League Championship Series Game 6
October 23, 2021 • Atlanta, Georgia
Braves 4, Dodgers 2

NATIONAL LEAGUE CHAMPIONS

Braves Advance to World Series for First Time Since 1999

By Gabriel Burns

The season that wasn't turned into the October that finally was.

After a two-decade absence, the Braves are back in the World Series for the first time this millennium. They eliminated the reigning champion Dodgers in the National League Championship Series, capped by a 4-2 victory in Game 6 in front of 43,060 fans at Truist Park.

"I'm not sure I'm feeling yet, honestly," manager Brian Snitker said after the game. "I'm kind of numb. Pretty good feeling, though. Just happy for the guys, the organization. (During the final out) I just kind of sat in my chair and them guys swamped me. There were a lot. I was just hoping I could hold it together because a lot comes at you after all the years and everything you go through. And now to be able to experience this, it's really something cool."

These Braves defied the odds every step of the way. It was one of their July newcomers, Eddie Rosario, who played the biggest role in getting the team into the Fall Classic. Rosario had perhaps the greatest postseason series in Braves history, collecting 14 hits. He appropriately delivered the big blow Saturday, smashing a three-run homer off Walker Buehler to put the Braves ahead for good.

It's been a storybook journey for the 2021 Braves, whose route to avenging their NLCS ousting a year ago went nothing like they could've imagined in March.

Their season started in Philadelphia, where the Braves were swept. They stayed below .500 until Aug. 6. During

that frustrating stretch, they lost several key contributors. Their chances at a fourth consecutive division crown seemed toast.

But that's the charm in these Braves. No matter how bleak the situation appears, they had an answer for it.

Young ace Mike Soroka never returned as expected. Catcher Travis d'Arnaud missed several months, forcing the Braves to go on a maddening catching carousel. Outfielder Marcell Ozuna was injured then arrested on domestic-violence charges, ending his season. MVP candidate Ronald Acuna tore his ACL one day before the All-Star break. Early season star Huascar Ynoa broke his hand punching a bench. Every starter except Charlie Morton landed on the injured list.

"This whole year showed what the word resilience means from pretty much day one," first baseman Freddie Freeman said. "We just kept getting back up and just kept hitting punches back. That's just the collective whole as a unit that we have. It's just these guys, after last year, you could just taste it. We let it get away losing the 3-1 lead (in the 2020 NLCS) and we came back and we had to deal with the questions and we took that down real fast and I think that's just the group we have and that's the character we have."

The recurring thought for months: Sometimes it's just not your year. Yet it turned out, after years upon years of postseason failures, this was the Braves team that figured it out. This was even the one that didn't blow the 3-1 lead, separating itself from recent Atlanta sports history.

Freddie Freeman raises his arms in triumph after the final out of the Braves' 4-2 win in Game 6. With the win, the Braves advanced to the World Series for the first time since 1999. (Hyosub Shin/The Atlanta Journal-Constitution)

General manager Alex Anthopoulos executed one of the greatest trade deadlines in MLB history. In July, he reshaped his roster with outfielders Joc Pederson, Jorge Soler, Rosario and Adam Duvall. It didn't just save his team's season; it helped turn a middling team into a pennant winner.

The Braves went 34-18 across August and September. They surged past the fading Mets and perpetually mediocre Phillies to win their fourth consecutive NL East crown. Their 88 wins were tied for the fewest in franchise history for a division winner.

That didn't matter. As Anthopoulos stressed at the trade deadline, you just have to get into the tournament and anything can happen.

"I'm going to go with yes," Freeman said when asked if it's safe it's one of the greatest trade deadlines in MLB history. "It's two different teams, really, from the first half to the second half, if you really look at it. And then it took I think it was around a month (until Rosario debuted). So we just had little weapons waiting in the wings all over the place and then we unleashed them and here we are sitting in the World Series."

As Freeman suggested, this was better than an 88-win team after the trades. The Braves faced the 95-win Brewers in their Division Series. They dropped Game 1 – giving them their necessary adversity – then won three straight, including a thriller in Game 4, to advance.

Meanwhile, the 107-win Giants and 106-win Dodgers squared off on the other end of the bracket. The Dodgers prevailed, setting up an NLCS rematch from a year ago, when the Braves blew a 3-1 lead to Los Angeles at the neutral Texas site then. The Dodgers went on to win their first title since 1988.

These Braves proved they're better than the team before them. They had home-field advantage, a benefit awarded to division winners - which the Dodgers weren't - and won the first two games on walk-off hits.

That sent them to Los Angeles, a house of horrors over the past decade. The theme continued in Game 3, when the Braves blew a 5-2 lead late and saw a team "dead in the water," according to Dodgers manager Dave Roberts, suddenly find life. It appeared they could be in danger of doing what Atlanta teams often do.

As these Braves have shown, they can't be compared with any other club. They responded to their missed opportunity in Game 3 by walloping the Dodgers in Game 4. The Dodgers, as

Eddie Rosario hoists the NLCS MVP trophy after the Braves' clinching Game 6 win over the Dodgers. Rosario went 14-for-25 (.560) with a double, triple, three home runs and nine RBIs in the series. (Curtis Compton/The Atlanta Journal-Constitution)

one would expect from the champions, didn't go quietly. They crushed the Braves 11-2 in Game 5, forcing the series back to Atlanta.

"#KillTheNarrative," the Braves tweeted. They embraced Atlanta sports' track record, then backed up their words. This time, the Braves didn't blow a 3-1 lead. They didn't even let it reach a Game 7.

"I think this might be the definition of pure joy," Freeman said.

Ian Anderson, who started Game 7 against the Dodgers last year, allowed one run over four innings. His offense backed him up and he won the latest biggest game in his career this time. Anderson started the team's division-clinching win and Game 7 this season.

Rosario was named NLCS MVP. His 14 hits included three home runs, and he had nine RBIs. He homered twice in Game 4, helping the Braves gain a 3-1 series advantage. His home run in Game 6 was the difference in the deciding contest.

"I always knew that I could win an MVP trophy like this," Rosario said via team interpreter Franco Garcia. "It was something I always hoped for, regardless of what anyone said or thought of me. But I want more. Also, this is obviously my greatest accomplishment of my career so far, this trophy and this award, so it's something to definitely be proud of."

The Dodgers' best scoring chance was the seventh. The Dodgers had three reach against Luke Jackson, cutting their deficit to 4-2 with runners at second and third.

Enter Tyler Matzek, who struck out Albert Pujols, Steven Souza and Mookie Betts. Matzek has come through countless times during the Braves' run - eight of his nine postseason appearances were scoreless and he's appeared in all but one contest - but none were more crucial than Saturday.

"Both of those guys could have been co-MVPs for me," Anthopoulos said of Rosario and Matzek. Lefty A.J. Minter, who pitched two scoreless innings in two games over the series, added: "Eddie had an unbelievable series, but in my opinion, Matzek was the MVP."

That this Braves team, flawed, frustrated and wounded for so much of the year, was the one to achieve what so many before it couldn't, is a testament to baseball's beauty and randomness. As AJC columnist

Mark Bradley worded it: This isn't the best Braves team, but it might be the right one.

No Acuna. No Ozuna. No Soroka. None of the Braves' starting outfielders in the NLCS were on their opening-day roster. The makeshift group is now four wins from immortality.

"Going from 97 losses six years ago to doing this, it's special," Freeman said. "And to lose, in my opinion, the best player in the National League (Acuna) and we're up here going to the World Series, it's amazing what this team did."

The 2021 Braves could win the franchise's second championship since moving to Atlanta in 1966. They're playing for that honor for the first time since the glorified 1990s Braves made their last Fall Classic appearance in 1999. They won 10 division titles and made 12 postseason appearances between World Series berths.

This was a franchise that went 19 years without winning a postseason series before last October. Within two weeks, it could be one that's scheduled to get fitted for rings.

Saturday's result evoked endless emotions, be it from a mainstay like first baseman Freddie Freeman or a newcomer like Rosario, who hadn't experienced a postseason series victory before this month. Snitker has waited longest. An over four-decade long career with the Braves has culminated with a World Series berth.

Next, the Braves will face the Astros for the championship. Troy Snitker, Brian's son, is a hitting coach for Houston.

"The Snitkers are going to have a World Series trophy in their house here," Brian said. "I don't know who is going to own it, but we're going to have one."

Like their series against the Brewers and Dodgers, the Braves aren't favored in the World Series. The mighty Astros are on a torrid roll, trying to capture a championship without an asterisk (their 2017 title was tainted by a cheating scandal). Houston's offense will present quite the challenge for Braves pitching.

The Braves will embrace the underdog role yet again. Why wouldn't they? It's worked for them the entire season. They've overcome everything imaginable to reach this stage. The Astros won't be intimidating. ■

Eddie Rosario's three-run home run off of Dodgers starter Walker Buehler in the fourth inning gave the Braves all the runs they would need in Atlanta's 4-2 victory. (Curtis Compton/The Atlanta Journal-Constitution)

Ozzie Albies celebrates after hitting a two-out double in the first inning of Game 6 of the NLCS against the Dodgers. Albies later came around to score the game's first run on an Austin Riley double. (Curtis Compton/The Atlanta Journal-Constitution)